"This 'evergreen' book contains a wealth of valuable and timeless ideas, gems of information, strategies and tactics you will find yourself referring to again and again. It will empower you with the tools to succeed in a highly competitive selling environment."
—WILLIAM O. MEHNERT, CEO, STRATEGIC LEARNING, INC.

"This is essential reading for anyone who wants to take their game to the next level, for anyone who wants to excel. It is a book that is easy to read and easy to follow, with a logical flow. From page one to the closing comments, it struck home with me."
—STEVE CARLSON, SALES PROFESSIONAL

"If every sales professional were to follow the principles outlined in this book we would have fewer cranky customers and no cranky companies! Jim DeSena provides a valuable process for anyone who wants to be an exceptional sales leader, because before we can sell we must be sold on service."
—C. LESLIE CHARLES, AUTHOR OF *WHY IS EVERYONE SO CRANKY?* AND *THE CUSTOMER SERVICE COMPANION*

THE 10 IMMUTABLE LAWS OF POWER SELLING

The Key to Winning Sales, Wowing Customers, and Driving Your Profits Through the Roof

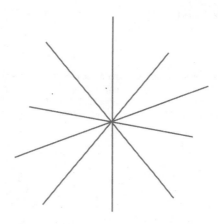

JAMES DeSENA

McGraw·Hill

New York   Chicago   San Francisco   Lisbon   London   Madrid   Mexico City
Milan   New Delhi   San Juan   Seoul   Singapore   Sydney   Toronto

Library of Congress Cataloging-in-Publication Data

DeSena, James A.
    Take the lead and win : 10 imperatives for becoming top sales producer in any
market / James A. DeSena.
         p.   cm.
    Includes bibliographical references and index.
    ISBN 0-07-141661-7
    1. Selling.   I. Title.

    HF5438.25.D464   2003
    658.85—dc21   2003045945

1 2 3 4 5 6 7 8 9 0   AGM/AGM   2 1 0 9 8 7 6 5 4 3

ISBN 0-07-141661-7

McGraw-Hill books are available at special quantity discounts to use as premiums and
sales promotions, or for use in corporate training programs. For more information, please
write to the Director of Special Sales, Professional Publishing, McGraw-Hill, Two Penn
Plaza, New York, NY 10121-2298. Or contact your local bookstore.

This book is printed on acid-free paper.

To those with courage

CONTENTS

PREFACE

Adapt or perish, now as ever, is nature's inexorable imperative.
—H. G. WELLS

Stand Out and Survive

Standing out in a crowded sales arena isn't easy. Customers are more demanding than ever. Product or service advantages don't last long. Competition comes from unexpected places. A soft economy makes for a tougher sale. Finding new and better ways to serve customers is a battle you must win each day. Sales leaders do.

Sales leaders are sales professionals who help their customers take advantage of change by creating a vision of a customer solution and inspiring others to help them deliver it.

Sales leaders have the courage to act in the face of uncertainty, to create confidence in place of doubt, and to inspire others to follow their lead in the solutions they create with their customers. Sales leaders are adept at meeting new challenges. They expand possibilities. They create excitement.

There Has Been an Underappreciated Shift in the Nature of Sales

The landscape has changed. Technology, information, communication, globalization, and consolidation have changed the marketplace dramatically and will continue to do so. To excel in this environment, sales professionals must adopt new strategies. Sales leaders are defined by their willingness and ability to do so.

Some salespeople continue to practice old-style sales tactics (high pressure, little understanding of customer needs, too much talking). Why? Old habits are hard to break. Salespeople who use them don't realize how aware most customers are of those tactics.

But even salespeople who work honestly without pressuring customers are still vulnerable because of the vastness and speed of the information-rich Internet. Salespeople who only provide pricing or information and take orders are destined to become the dinosaurs of the information age. They can be replaced by automated ordering systems. Customers don't like wasting time with salespeople who don't add value to the buying process, and when the sale is for what are considered standard items, customers are eager to streamline the process.

Streamlining the sales process isn't any different from streamlining other processes inside progressive organizations. Companies have sought to cut response time, reduce costs, and eliminate duplication. Huge sales opportunities will always be available to salespeople who go after them. (We have examples in this book from sales organizations recognized as being among the best from sources such as *Selling Power* magazine.) These top sales producers win these sales by leading, not by following.

Sales professionals who want to continue to be successful *will* realize that the world isn't the same today as it was yesterday. They know they must adapt to it. Sales professionals have to take the lead in applying new strategies that capitalize on change. They need to lead that change through their customers' and their own organizations. That is the only way to maintain a leadership position. Sales leaders must operate as the most successful and lasting businesses do: evolve to meet new demands and opportunities. Sales leaders know how to deal with change and turn it to their advantage.

Effective salespeople also realize that it isn't just the *number* of sales calls they make that counts, but the *quality* of those calls. Are they calling on the right companies, at the right levels, with the right products and the right strategies? Do they create high value for the customer with their problem solving? It is a matter of being effective as opposed to being efficient—to provide the right products to the right customers and develop relationships that grow business.

This book is for sales professionals who want to be exceptional in this new environment. The sales leaders' model (figure 1) shows that sales professionals solve problems and create high value for their customers and that leaders capitalize on change with innovative thinking and approaches. *Sales leaders* focus on both of these challenges: they solve problems in an environment of rapid change, creating both high value *and* innovative customer solutions. Most sales professionals still face a daily test to find new ways to meet their sales quotas, broaden their customer base, and stabilize their sales revenues. This book provides a fresh approach for overcoming such challenges and offers a unique perspective on sales and leadership for salespeople who want to stand out in their field.

The salespeople who survive and prosper in the future will be those who not only have a good foundation of selling skills, but who are able to deliver high-value, innovative solutions that build lasting customer

Figure 1 Sales Leaders' Model

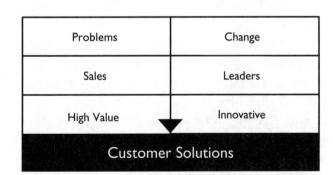

relationships and success in an environment of rapid change. This book provides the leadership strategies that will help you accomplish that.

Donald and Doris Fisher founded Gap Inc. in 1969, in San Francisco, California, with a single store and a few employees. They opened the store because they couldn't find jeans that fit well. Today, Gap has evolved into three brands and one of the world's largest specialty retailers, with sales of $3.35 billion, 165,000 employees, and 4,250 stores in 3,100 locations in the United States, United Kingdom, Canada, France, Japan, and Germany as of this writing. What Donald and Doris Fisher did is what sales leaders do: be alert for problems and then look for or create solutions.

The 10 Immutable Laws of Power Selling presents a new model for successfully selling in an environment of rapid change. POWER, in the context of the sales leaders' model, means to:

Produce High-Value,
Own the Innovative Solution, and
Win with
Exceptional
Results

To be successful in a constantly changing and highly competitive marketplace, you must be a leader. To do anything less is to leave your fate in someone else's hands. If you are not the one finding and solving new customer problems, someone else will be.

Why I Wrote This Book

Over the last fifteen years, I have had the opportunity to advise some of the finest sales organizations in the U.S. and Canada. I have met and worked with thousands of salespeople—rookies, veterans, and leaders in their field. I enjoy working with them. They are inquisitive, energizing, and challenging. Most salespeople have a thirst for learning. They enjoy a good dialogue, and most continually seek ways to serve their customers better. I have learned something from each of them. They appreciate good ideas and relevant information.

The leadership models and recommendations presented in this book uniquely capture the methods that allow top sales producers to take advantage of the opportunities that come with rapid change. The 10 Laws are the result of years of field-tested best practices from thousands of sales professionals. I'm sure you will find the information it contains to be invaluable in dramatically growing your business.

What You Can Expect from This Book

The information contained in this book is the result of seventeen years of work, beginning with my research into understanding sales and sales management competency (what it takes to successfully sell) when I was a marketing manager at AT&T. The book is not as much about selling techniques as it is about how to be effective and innovative and sell successfully for the long term. It is about leadership—doing the right things and inspiring others to follow.

Part I, "Make the Sale," is about how to deliver high-value solutions in the right markets. Its focus is not how many calls to make but rather how to make the right calls. Much more than a primer on basic selling techniques, it encourages salespeople who want to be leaders in their industry to define their businesses in customers' terms and determine the specific advantages they bring to the market. It suggests that leaders consider their business model because that model may ultimately determine how quickly the business will succeed, or perhaps whether it will succeed at all. It provides recommendations for identifying the problems you can solve for your customers and then effectively positioning that message with them and delivering on your promises. It is about winning sales, building relationships, and keeping customers.

Part II, "Take the Lead," provides a framework for sales leaders who create innovative solutions for their customers. It is about leading change in a sales environment. Building on Part I, it takes leadership from selling in the right markets with the right products and right positioning into understanding and challenging the status quo. It distinguishes between the concepts of management and leadership. It examines how exceptional sales leaders are able to define limits and then exceed them to deliver innovative customer solutions. It is about how to change the framework and make unique and larger sales.

Part III, "Win," suggests that to be a leader for the long term requires a number of traits, such as integrity, planning, and balance. Integrity involves trust. Planning means identifying and staying with the right priorities and using time wisely; it helps you avoid the management-by-crisis mentality that can undermine your effectiveness and distract from high-value customer activities. Balance is about understanding the ultimate benefits that sales leaders can attain, depending on how they view themselves and why they do what they do.

This Book Is for You

This book is for successful sales professionals who would like to understand why they are successful and to initiate small changes that can make them even more successful. It is for successful salespeople who would like to be more focused and productive and win larger sales. It is for successful salespeople who would like to attain greater satisfaction in their personal relationships with their families so as to realize the total benefits of their career.

This book is for sales vice presidents who would like to instill a systematic sales approach for creating high-value, innovative customer solutions. It is for new or aspiring salespeople who would like to become leaders in their field. It is for sales managers who would like to coach salespeople to be leaders in their field.

If you are reading this, you are serious about your career. If you want to be exceptional, this book is for you.

How to Get the Most from This Book

This book contains a wealth of ideas, information and inspiration. Here are my recommendations for how you can benefit the most from this book.

First, glance through the table of contents. It will give you a good understanding of what is covered in each chapter. Then select which of the three parts of the book you wish to begin with and read each of the laws within that part.

I like the format of Harvey Mackay's book *Swim with the Sharks* because its short chapters allow you to read in small bites. I designed this book so that it would be fast reading, even though with the scope of information it covers, you won't read it at a single sitting. But you will find that you won't go for more than a couple of pages before you come to a new topic. You can pick up the book and read almost any page or two and get a snapshot of self-contained useful information. I've also relied on lists, tables, and quotes to provide a change a pace as you read, so you should find yourself looking forward to turning to the next page. You'll also find what I call the core of the law at the end of each chapter that discusses one of the 10 laws.

Talk about what most interests you with your colleagues, sales associates, or sales manager. Implement a new idea and then judge how well it works for you. Assess your current level of effectiveness and decide how you would like to take it to the next level.

Becoming an Exceptional Sales Professional

The two things that salespeople must do are to sell and to keep customers happy. It's not complicated, but it's not easy. One of my assignments while at AT&T involved designing a sales competency model. We wanted some way of assuring ourselves that our salespeople could sell effectively. We wanted to know we could relied on them to consistently deliver results that we and customers wanted. We were especially concerned about preventing mistakes by identifying the skills or knowledge they needed ahead of time.

Until we developed this competency model, we did as most companies did. We hired people. We sent them to a sales training course and did other training from time to time. We assigned them a territory. We gave them a manager. We gave them sales goals.

Their territories were large, which meant that the sales manager didn't get to spend much time with each salesperson. So we weren't sure that they were doing the job as well as they could be doing it. Yes, we could measure results, but could the objectives have been higher and still have been realistic? Were they even the right objectives? We really wanted to be sure the salespeople were competent to do the job.

So we developed a competency model. This model started with the two results we wanted from our salespeople, sales and customer satisfaction, and worked backward from there. If the salespeople had to be able to make a quality sale and maintain customer satisfaction, what specific skills and knowledge would they need in order to do that? How would we measure their skill level in each area? How would we develop those areas that were weaker? What type of person would best match the job? Those were the questions we started with to develop the competency model.

Bear in mind that competency is a lot like fluency in a foreign language. You can take a language course in school, but that doesn't mean you are fluent. Just because you know something doesn't mean you can do it well. When you represent your product or service and your company, you don't want to take a chance and find out you are not "fluent" in some important skill or product knowledge area. You lose credibility, which is costly.

When I've asked sales managers for the profile of their best performers, they described them in the following ways.

- *The best performers have a wide range of contacts within the account.* They develop those multiple points of contact to expand or protect the business. They communicate with people at various levels in the organization, not just at the contact level (management, executive, and professional), and with people in various functions (engineering, finance, or product development, for example).
- *The best performers take initiative.* They take responsibility and ownership without being asked to do so. They don't ignore issues; they take action. They drive business decisions.

- *The best performers understand business, not just sales.* They work to come up with solutions that address the customer's business issues. They know how to put together a business "deal."
- *The best performers are good communicators.* They communicate with a variety of people. They get their message across, making sure it is not misunderstood or lost. They are excited about what they do and are convinced that it is the right thing to do for the customer. They don't rely on force to get things done, but are diplomatically persistent in getting people to act quickly.
- *The best performers have a positive attitude.* They may face obstacles, but they believe they can achieve their objectives in spite of those obstacles, or even because of them. They rarely (if ever) complain, whine, or commiserate; they are more likely to act to change a situation they don't like. They tend to have a good outlook on life in general, are able to look at the big picture when they need to, and often have a sense of humor that helps people feel at ease. One sales manager told me that in Europe they call it *charisma*. No matter where you are or what you call it, it works.

This is the profile of someone who is highly competent in a range of important skills: a leader. It's someone who not only makes the sale, but influences others to follow their lead to accomplish great things.

What is your competency level? How do you know? Could it be improved? What new knowledge or skills do you need to keep pace with product, technology, and industry changes? Could your attitude be improved? How much time are you willing to invest in developing professionally? Are you willing to critically evaluate your effectiveness and accept feedback? These are some of the questions exceptional sales professionals answer and act on.

If you want to be among the world's sales leaders, you will find a treasure trove of strategies contained in these pages. Use them and expect exceptional results.

ACKNOWLEDGMENTS

There are many people I would like to thank for their help, insight, and guidance in writing this book. First are the people to whom this book is dedicated, my family, whose support, love, and real-world lessons gave life to this book: my wife, Terry, who has been by my side as my life partner, my alter ego, and my wise counselor, seeing things that I couldn't see; my daughter Trier, who helped with the original outline and assembly of material and whose work as an elementary schoolteacher inspires me and gives lifelong learning to the children in her classes; my daughter Jamie, who has proofed and edited many documents for me and whose quick insights have always been remarkable; and my mother, Evelyn, who has been an ardent advocate and whose vision of me as an author was gratifying. She is a fighter who never gives up on life.

Thank-you to the clients I have had the opportunity to serve. One of the things I enjoy most about my work is the people I meet. Thanks also to the many sales leaders I have had the privilege to work with. Their dedication to their field and their development and openness to learning and sharing is an asset that not only provided many of the examples in this book, but fuels our economy by bringing high-value, innovative solutions to customers. Without those solutions, there would be no progress.

Thank-you also to the following people who were instrumental in helping bring this book into being: George Gulla; Tim Polk; Tony Alessandra, PhD, CPAE, CSP; Linda Bolton; Bill Brooks, CSP, CPAE;

Paula Davis; Gil Eagles, CSP, CPAE; Molly Faust; Tom Hausman; Steve Jasper; Susan Giuseppetti; Gordon Lambourne; Frank Pitt; Mark Riesenberg; Judy Shaffer; Cyndi Walsh; and Steve Wojnarowicz. Thanks to Craig Bolt at McGraw-Hill. A special thanks to Barry Neville, my editor at McGraw-Hill for his guidance and insights. Thank-you to each person who played a role in helping me to develop or write this book.

PART I

MAKE THE SALE

FOUR STRATEGIES FOR PRODUCING HIGH-VALUE SOLUTIONS AND BUILDING LASTING CUSTOMER RELATIONSHIPS

Law 1: Create High Value
Law 2: Decide on Your Market
Law 3: Develop Customer Expertise in Your Market
Law 4: Build Relationships for Repeat Business

"Our philosophy is to sell the way the customer wants to buy."
—John W. Marriott III, executive vice president,
lodging, Marriott International

Think of Your Own Buying Experience

Think about the best and worst buying experiences you've ever had. What did the salesperson do to make it a good experience? What did the salesperson do to make it a bad one?

Isn't it easier to remember the worst experience? When we have bad buying experiences, what do we do? We often make an emotional vow never to do business with that individual or company again.

What contributes to the worst experiences? Customers say such things as:

- Not listening
- High pressure
- Talking down to me, being rude
- Selling me a less than ideal solution and not telling me
- Not doing or delivering what was promised

What contributes to the best experiences?

- Listening and learning about me, being prepared, knowing my situation
- Declining to sell me something that isn't right
- Doing more than expected
- Helping me be a more educated buyer

You might know what it takes to be the best, but do you have the motivation to do it? Do you appreciate the benefits? Do you have the time to do it? Do you know how? There is a huge void between knowing something and doing it, between doing something and doing it well.

Sales leaders strive to be the best. They don't settle for less. They don't want their customers to settle for less than the best, either. Sales leaders take the initiative to continually improve. Leadership starts with initiative. It relies on being willing to make changes and to take risks in new areas. Sales leaders take no comfort in the status quo. They know the comfort it brings is fleeting.

The Model

Sales leaders have carefully thought through the principles on which their business is founded. (And they do look at what they do as a business.) They have answered these three fundamental questions:

- *Why* are you in business?
- *What* do you want to accomplish?
- *How* do you plan on doing it?

They also execute their plans extremely well, attending carefully to details and taking into account the uncertainties of future projections and the quirky contingencies that can arise.

I call the model I'm going to describe here *market-based selling* (figure 2). The model is designed specifically for the sales professional. It is based on the belief that before you sell, you must be clear about whom you are selling to and why. Companies must successfully market their products and services in order to survive. As a sales professional, you must market yourself successfully to stand out from the crowd. Prospecting is about developing the market you've identified. Selling is

Figure 2

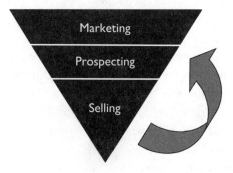

about getting in front of the customer. What happens if one "link" is missing? Simple: no commission check.

If you haven't identified the people you want to market to, how will you find them? If you don't prospect, whom will you sell to? You will be at the behest of whatever business happens to come your way based on existing customers, which could be good but may not be enough and will diminish over time.

Defining your market is about finding the right prospects. This is more about quality than quantity. Prospecting and cold calling depend on numbers—it's all about quantity. The more people you get in front of, the more chances you have to sell. Selling is about finding the right problems, the ones customers are feeling. When you are in front of customers, it isn't about numbers—it's about preparation and planning, about asking the right questions.

The arrow in figure 2 shows that you must get feedback from your customers. Sales professionals must seek feedback from customers in order to know what they are doing right and what they need to improve, just as companies do.

The concept behind this model is that the best salespeople are good not only at selling, but at marketing. They understand who their customers are and what they have to offer them that is unique or special. They understand how to position themselves with their market to take maximum advantage of their strategic strengths. Sales leaders blend the marketing and sales function. They place a lot of emphasis on understanding their market before they start selling to it. They are also adept at working with their marketing people to develop special features or products to meet customer needs.

Top producers don't rely on high-pressure tactics. Instead, they *earn* the customer's business by understanding the customer, the customer's industry, and the customer's customers. They build trusting relationships with customers and help them solve problems and take advantage of opportunities. They understand which customers they serve best and how to serve them. Serving customers well requires continually improving. This might sound straightforward and easy, but it takes critical self-evaluation, commitment, self-discipline, and continuous training and learning.

This book is designed to provide information, examples, and opportunities you can apply and personalize to your business. It is designed to be practical so that you can get the information you need quickly. Developing well-considered answers to the questions the book poses and then applying them consistently will help you improve sales effectiveness, income, and profits.

The three elements of this model, which are explored in Part I and shown in figure 3, include the following:

- **_Discipline_**, which describes how to _deliver high-value solutions_
- **_Direction_**, which describes how to _decide on a market_
- **_Depth_**, which describes how to _develop expertise in your market_

The first element of the model, discipline, will help you be clear about what value is in specific forms and in the customer's eyes.

The second element of the model, direction, will help you be clear about who your best customers are and how you can deliver high-value solutions to them.

The third element of the model, depth, will allow you to become highly knowledgeable about the customer's business, comprehending it

Figure 3

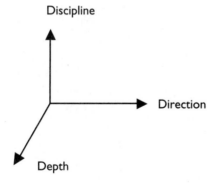

from a different perspective, and even understanding it better than the customer does in some respects.

Because you're in sales, you've found things that work for you. Keep on doing them. You've probably also found some things that don't work quite as well as you would like. This book will help you understand why the things that work well for you work the way they do and what you can do to change the things that aren't working so well.

"People value you at the value you are seen to put on yourself."

—Cindy Gallop, president and chief operating officer, Bartle Bogle Hegarty

CREATE HIGH VALUE

If you are going to deliver high value to your customers, the first thing you need to do is to solve their problems.

What Problems Do You Solve for Your Customers?

Selling is about solving customer problems, whether those are problems they are currently facing or problems they will face as their marketplace evolves and their needs change. When I asked a top sales professional about what he did that allowed him to stand out in his field, he responded very simply, "I solve problems." Simple, but not easy.

If you can't put your finger on your customer's problem, you won't solve it. Worse, you will waste time and lose credibility. You must describe the problem clearly, and do it from the customer's point of view. The problem should be one the customer sees value in solving. To find out what the really difficult problems are, ask the right questions and listen before acting.

The overarching problem, or goal, for most executives is how to make their businesses more profitable as quickly, reliably, and inexpensively as possible so that they can be assured that they will remain in business, keep the owners happy, and keep their jobs. Myriad other problems are related to that main concern; for example,

- Finding new customers
- Keeping existing customers

- Selling more to existing customers
- Improving customer service
- Reducing personnel costs
- Improving quality and reducing defects
- Reducing customer complaints
- Decreasing time to market
- Improving market share (or mind share)
- Taking advantage of new technology
- Improving morale
- Developing new products
- Leaving markets or closing units

The most successful salespeople are the ones who find pressing customer problems and do something to solve them in a way that is convenient, cost effective, or timely. Top salespeople find problems that customers are ready to solve, then work hard to solve them. Of course, finding those problems and then delivering good solutions for them requires a well-planned and organized effort. This book provides the steps for delivering high-value, innovative customer solutions and recommendations for identifying the customer's priorities for solving those problems.

Top sales professionals know that when you find customers' significant, pressing problems, they will be willing to pay for solutions. Finding those significant problems means sorting out customers who are ready and willing to buy from those who aren't. A critical success factor is how to market your problem-solving abilities so people know what you can do for them and how they can save time, money, or effort by using your solutions.

Taking the initiative to identify and solve customer-related problems in unique ways is leadership. Sales leaders open untapped and sometimes vast new market opportunities. What problems are you solving for your customers? If you were to ask your customers, what would they say? If you asked them to prioritize those problems, would there be any surprises? Customers have many problems. Find those that they want to solve the most and that you are uniquely qualified to solve, and you will have a winning combination.

So, how do you solve problems? There are proven problem-solving steps you can use. You may use them already. Let's take a look at one approach.

Five-Step Problem-Solving Approach

People who are really good at solving problems go about it systematically. They have a way of placing the problem in context. They don't jump to conclusions. They evaluate alternatives.

A good way to become a systematic problem solver is to adopt the following five-step problem-solving process.

1. *Identify the problem.* This is critical: you must try to solve the *right* problem. Don't try to solve a problem the customer sees as low priority or unimportant. Identify the right problem by asking the right questions and observing. You cannot identify the customer's problems by presenting your products. What's leading the customer to feel there is a problem? Is it something specific, or is it an intuitive sense that things aren't as they should be? Can the customer define the problem?

2. *Analyze the problem.* How often does the problem occur? How severe is it? Are there any special circumstances that are present when it occurs? What might be the causes of the problem? Can you rule out any causes? How long has it been going on? Has it gotten worse? How is the problem affecting other processes or people?

3. *Identify decision criteria.* How will you and the customer make decisions when it is time to decide? How will you weigh the criteria? Can you identify independent standards that can be used?

4. *Develop multiple solutions.* Don't stop at the first solution that you or others identify. It may be good, but much better ones may exist. Evaluate alternative scenarios. As objectively as possible, assess the pros and cons of each.

5. *Choose the optimal solution.* Use the criteria you developed in the third step of this problem-solving process to choose the best solu-

tion. Develop a base of support that will ensure you can implement the solution. Prepare for contingencies.

When you solve problems systematically, you save time, achieve better solutions, and increase your credibility with the customer and the perceived value of what you've done. If you can solve problems the customer is facing more expeditiously than someone else, the customer will appreciate the time saved.

Problem solving involves some considerations beyond those addressed by the five-step process. Once you have identified the problem you can sometimes rely on a known solution or a combination of known solutions. At other times, no ready solution is apparent. In that case, you may need to do a *business case analysis* to determine whether it will be profitable for your company to develop a solution. This includes asking what might be involved in developing the solution, how much time the process would require, and how well suited your company is to do the job. The issues become more complicated, but the problem-solving process may also be more rewarding.

You may need to tap into the knowledge you have acquired in solving similar or even dissimilar problems or the knowledge that exists in your company. You might need to have someone initiate research and create a solution from scratch (which can be cost prohibitive), or you can find a partner that already has the solution you need. You will need an innovative approach. Deciding to create solutions and driving them through the organization is part of what makes exceptional sales leaders exceptional.

An Example of Problem Analysis

Let's assume for the moment that a company wants its salespeople to improve their ability to uncover the high-priority problems the company's customers are facing and that they are not getting the information they need to do so. The reality is that there are a limited number of reasons people don't do what they are supposed to do.

- They don't know they should do it (caused by poor communication).
- The don't know how to do it (caused by a lack of skills).
- They don't want to do it (caused by a lack of motivation or a lack of rewards).
- Something keeps them from doing it (caused by a lack of resources or tools).

So if the company wants to change the skills, behaviors, and performance of its salespeople, the question is, what is the *reason* they aren't doing what they should or could be doing? Using the reasons listed, we can start to isolate the problem or problems. If the salespeople don't know how to identify customer problems, then training would be an appropriate solution. Most times, the issue isn't as simple as not knowing how to do something. Experienced salespeople already use a variety of skills, so it may be an issue of refining or advancing those skills. It may also be a case of changing habits that have developed over time, habits that interfere with doing the right things.

The salespeople may not want to do it because their managers don't approve of it when they do (a negative consequence). In this case, if they already know how to do it, the solution must involve working with the managers to gain their support or to provide them with the skills they need to understand customers' current needs. The idea is to use a systematic approach in isolating the problem. Don't rely on superficial observations.

Understand What Customers Value

When I say that sales leaders should deliver *high-value* solutions to customers, what do I mean? While it might be intuitively obvious, let's not leave this distinction to chance.

Value is what the customer determines it to be compared with available alternatives. It can be objective, subjective, or both. Objective measurements of value can be developed from cost savings or from revenue or profit increases. Determining exact amounts, even in these specific areas, can be difficult because relationships between revenue or profit increases and particular causes can be indistinct. And this process requires running tests, which aren't always practical. Absent exact amounts, estimates are better than no data.

What about subjective measurements of value? How much does the customer value the guarantee, for example? Or an extra level of service that you deliver? Or exclusivity? How does the customer prioritize or rate these?

If you can measure the value that customers derive from the products or services you sell, then you can reinforce the benefits of the particular products or services you sold them and gain insights that you can use to better sell high-value solutions to other customers.

Once you make a sale, if you reinforce the value of what you sold to the customer, you get three benefits. First, you increase the chances of retaining the customer and establish credibility with the customer that will likely generate repeat sales. Second, you find other areas in which you can help the customer. Third, you will be better able to find and sell to other customers who are looking for similar value.

In an article in the November-December 1998 issue of *Harvard Business Review*, James C. Anderson and James A. Narus advised that understanding what customers value is the most effective way to deliver the greatest possible value to customers. They suggest that an offering has two elements: its price and its value. Raising the price doesn't change the value. It changes the customer's incentive to purchase. Suppliers can demonstrate value by providing a case study to the customer after the solution has been implemented, relating the value realized to the solution proposed. Then they can draw on these case studies when making proposals to *new* customers. Knowing how customers value the elements of the product or service will also allow you to eliminate value "drains," as Anderson and Narus call them—services that cost you more to provide than they are worth to the customer.

For example, in a restaurant, most people want their server to pay attention to them without annoying them. Achieving the right balance is key, and eliminating some degree of communication would work to the server's advantage. The customer is the best one to tell you how often and in what form he or she prefers communication.

Create High-Value Solutions

One company that provided a great deal of price information on its website for car shoppers found that people got the information, then went to a local car dealer instead of clicking through in their site to order the car. The company was losing money on the site even though it was providing value. They concluded that they needed to get something of value before they gave it, so they did something simple: they reversed the screens. They asked people for information (in a way, qualified them) prior to getting the price quote. As a result, the company is now earning money on the site. The adage that people value less that which they receive for free may have been at work. When customers had to give some information, the perceived value of what they got increased. The company may not have had as many site visitors, but those who stayed bought.

Do customers perceive you as someone who is eager to sell to anyone, or as someone who provides products and services matched to their needs? Appearing too eager to make a sale makes people resistant to buying. Having some degree of exclusivity makes customers more eager to purchase. When you call for an appointment with a service professional and you can immediately get an appointment, don't you wonder why? If this person were good, wouldn't you have to wait?

Buy.com was faced with a similar situation. Buy.com was selling products at prices that were unprofitable, hoping to make up for those losses with advertising sales. That business model, as many dot-coms found out, doesn't work as well as it sounds. Buy.com decided it needed to raise prices, but at the same time keep customers raving about the value they received.

"To remain viable, we needed to create raving-fan clients who'd stay loyal as prices climbed," said Tom Silvell, vice president of customer support, as reported by Ginger Cooper in the November 2001 issue of *CRM Magazine* (p. 34). Silvell reviewed every part of the customer experience. Using customer relationship management tools, they were able to cut order time, return time, and costs. The quality of the customer experience improved. And service ratings went up dramatically. Silvell said, "We built our programs and technologies around what customers wanted and needed instead of letting our programs and technologies drive their behavior. This tactic helped transition us from a price-sensitive shop to one focused on the customer experience, on offering value to clients, and on providing quality merchandise at reasonable prices."

A study conducted by the Gartner Group, also reported in the same issue of *CRM Magazine*, found that less than 5 percent of companies worldwide have successfully implemented what they call a "customer-centric" approach. A company may think it focuses on the customer, but likely still has much room for improvement.

What is your perspective as a sales professional? What is the customer's buying experience when buying from you? Is it convenient and efficient? How do you know? If you don't, now would be a good time to find out.

Business Models

What is your business model? How well does it work? How do you find and serve customers? A business model is simply a way of describing what your business does and how it does it. An aspect of recent business models, for example, is the channel for reaching customers. Do you sell directly or through others? Do you use fixed pricing, contracts, or negotiated pricing?

There has been much discussion lately about business models, prompted by the application of the Internet to new ways of reaching and selling to customers. The unfortunate downside to some Internet businesses is that their models overlooked the need to produce profits. The assumption was that investors would tolerate long-term losses almost indefinitely, as long as the promise of future profits fueled an increasing stock price. But the bubble burst when the underlying demand evaporated and investors sought companies that were producing or had demonstrated that they would produce profits in the future.

Even having a compelling vision for a business model and deep-pocketed investors is no guarantee of success, as Global Crossings proved in early 2002. Their vision was to create a global fiber optic network, but they had trouble signing up enough customers to fund the huge investment. The importance of the business model in this case, and with so many dot-com businesses, was that the model has to factor in profitable sales. Unrestrained growth leads to unrealistic sales requirements that place salespeople in untenable positions.

One company I worked with refused to compete with their customers; it was an important component of their business model. This particular client of mine sold products to other businesses, which then sold the products to end users. The client could have tried to sell directly to the end users, a practice that would essentially have amounted to competing with their own customers. Some of the client's competitors did, but this business chose not to. This proposition gave the company a beneficial selling advantage that could position them uniquely with customers.

Individual salespeople operate with sales models that may be effective or ineffective. To maximize effectiveness, they need to think about how they will reach their potential customers. For example, you might try something as simple as sales materials that describe your qualifications, experience, present customers, results you've achieved for your customers, testimonials, and contact information.

> *"Our site followed many of the existing conventions. It had a lot of information and had lots of buy now buttons. What it did not do was follow our sales model. We got bogged down in features and functions, instead of outcomes and emotions."*
>
> —Mike Manning, director of e-commerce,
> *Hooked on Phonics*

Deliver Consistent Value

Consistency is firmness of constitution or character. Customers value consistency, even at the expense of higher value. They want to be sure about what they are receiving; they don't like negative surprises. When you deliver consistent value, you increase the perceived value of your product or service.

The following three leadership strategies will help you consistently deliver on the promise of value.

- *Make decisions consistent with your goals and values.* People tend to encounter difficulty when they make decisions inconsistent with their goals or values—those things that are really important to them, their company, their customers, or their loved ones. How we make important decisions can be as important as the decisions themselves. Every decision brings consequences. With important decisions, the consequences can be far-reaching.
- *Produce results consistently.* Customers come to have certain expectations. When those expectations aren't met, they are disappointed, especially if their expectations are higher of you than they are of others. The adage "Underpromise and overdeliver" is the key. Have just a little something extra in reserve so that you don't exceed expectations one time and not meet them the next time. Build in a cushion, especially when it comes to cost and schedules.
- *Behave consistently.* People judge us based on our behaviors, not our intentions. Inconsistent or unpredictable behaviors make it difficult for other people to know how to best work with us, or, more important, whether they can even trust us. It makes it difficult for people to plan.

Trust is rooted in the assurance that someone will do something they say they will do. It is a driving force in relationships, especially ones involving customers. Their reputations, and sometimes their jobs, are at stake. While trust isn't easily measured, you can be sure it underlies our motives and our responses.

What are the attributes of a sales relationship with high trust levels? Good communication, innovative thinking, and a lack of hidden agendas. Customers who trust salespeople provide good information, take the advice of salespeople, and give them the opportunity to keep their business.

Surveys have shown that when people travel, what they value most in a hotel is consistency. Whether it is a luxury or economy brand, they want the accommodations and services to be the same every time they return. People who go to their favorite fast-food restaurant want the same level of service no matter which location they visit. The same is true for most of us with the products or services we purchase. We value consistency. So do, of course, our customers.

Reinforce Value

Make sure you reinforce the value you provide to your existing customers, especially when budgets tighten up. The customer may not recognize the value that may be apparent to you. If you take it for granted that the customer understands everything that you do to deliver value and you are mistaken, the customer may make decisions that will be difficult for you to reverse once they are made. It is better to be proactive by understanding what your customers' value perceptions are and communicating with them early in the process about that value.

The Core of Law 1: Deliver High Value

Identify the problems and opportunities unique to your customers and then create what they consider high-value solutions.

DECIDE ON YOUR MARKET

Here are five of the most important questions you must answer about your business.

- What do you do for your customers?
- Who are your customers?
- Why do they buy?
- Why should they buy from your company?
- How do you negotiate price?

Let's look at the first one.

What Do You Do for Your Customers?

This may be the single most important question you must answer to be successful. Define your answer not in terms of activities, but of results—results that are important to your customers. For example, staffing (such as providing temporary employees) is an activity. But results for the customer would include lower staffing costs and absenteeism, higher quality output and greater productivity, reliability, getting qualified people quickly, and a highly motivated, flexible workforce.

You should focus on results that differentiate you from everyone else. Standing out in a world of many choices is critical to your success. Regardless of what you do, at some level you are delivering results to others. Your success will depend on how those people perceive the value of the results you deliver and how unique those results are. Being clear about what it is you really do for your customers is the only way you can deliver it. You must answer the question about what value you bring to the customer, what you add that wouldn't otherwise be there, and why that is important to the customer.

When I first went out on my own, someone asked me what I did. I responded with "I'm a consultant," and as I said it I unconsciously raised my shoulders. I realized later that I had raised my shoulders because I really didn't have a specific idea of what I was going to do. Being a consultant covers a wide spectrum. In my former job, being a generalist was a good thing. But if I was going to solve customer problems, I needed to focus: what type of problems would I solve, and for what type of customers?

Value Propositions

A *value proposition* is a statement of the value you promise to deliver to a customer who purchases your products or services. It is the unique set of benefits you can deliver to a customer; it's the list of reasons the customer should buy the product or service. Because it proposes a promise, I recommend you think of a value proposition as a *value promise*, the promise of the value you will deliver to the customer. Thinking of this as a promise positions it in your mind with the weight it deserves. The value you promise becomes paramount in directing all of your efforts to meet that promise.

A customer picks a specific product or service because of the value he or she thinks will result from that choice. The customer may or may not see all of the results as valuable, but will make the purchase if there is a favorable or compelling reason to select the seller at that time. Value is in the eye of the beholder and is very much dependent on the customer's circumstances and experiences. Value isn't limited to monetary results. The customer can value different aspects of your product or service, such as reliability, convenience, ease of use, or durability. The value that you add as an individual to the service is another part of the picture. The customer can value these attributes individually or in combination. Your value proposition should clearly explain what you do for your customers and what makes you unique or different from other suppliers.

More than anything else, a value proposition can help a company focus on what it really does for its customers and what those customers really want. It is a way of thinking clearly about what the customer's priorities are. If a value proposition is based only on the seller's views about what is important to customers, it may miss the mark. A technology company may see its value as delivering technology, but do their customers see that? Or do the customers see beyond the technology to other results? The perceived value will also depend on who the customer is in an organization.

Here are three points to consider in defining your value proposition:

- What do you do to solve customer problems?
- How are your solutions special or unique?
- What is your promise?

Keep in mind that value relates not only to the tangible and intangible benefits of your product or service but also to what your product or service does for the customer personally. That is often more important than other factors when the customer makes a purchase decision. If my job depends on whom I select as a vendor, how I think your solution will help me personally will be high on my list of considerations when I make a decision to select a vendor. I may not let others know of this, but it will be relevant. For example, the customer may want to be perceived in any of a number of ways by his or her organization: proactive, cost or quality conscious, a leader, or a tough negotiator.

You must be able to understand and communicate to your customers the value that you bring. A well-conceived value proposition is instrumental to customer satisfaction and loyalty and company profitability and growth. Well-planned communication is essential for you to create and sell a compelling proposition for the value you bring to customers.

One senior executive at a major company has a unique method for providing prospective representatives with his company's value proposition. Rather than simply telling them what it is, he asks them what they would expect in a relationship with a company that they would want to be associated with. They usually cite such desirable qualities as quick response time, competitive policies, strong service, and stable pricing. The executive then responds that they have exactly described his company's value proposition and then invites them to call any of the other representatives in his network. This company is quite selective in choosing representatives because it wants to maintain an extremely high level of service and it looks for the same level of commitment from its representatives.

> *"Great value-added propositions in this world start not from liberty and license but from need and want and hunger. Breakthroughs come from limits."*
> —Paul Hawken, cofounder and chairman, Groxis; also founder of Erewhon Trading Company, Smith & Hawken, and Metacode

What is it you do for your customers? What results do you get for them? Do you have a value proposition or have you in some way described the results from the customer's point of view? If not, there is no better time than now to begin to describe your value proposition. Be sure to distinguish between the activity and the result. Describe an activity, then a corresponding result.

Who Are Your Customers?

Are you going after the same customers as everyone else? Or are you serving a different market? Who are your best customers and which ones do you serve well? Some customers are profitable: they are easy and satisfying to work with, they make decisions quickly, they pay on time, and they give referrals and return on the time you invest.

Looking at the best of your current customers, the ones you have been most successful with, will give you a good idea about the type of customer you should seek in the future. If you don't have much of a customer base because you have just gotten started, think about what the ideal customer would be like.

What would a profile of *your* best customer look like?

- Positions (executive, manager, supervisor, consumer)
- Type of customer (business, consumer, nonprofit, government—if business, commercial or industrial)
- Location
- Geographic reach (local, state, national, international)
- Size (for example, less than 50 employees, 50 to 250 employees, 250 to 1,000 employees, and so on)
- Growth mode (high growth, low growth, retrenching)
- Technology (high tech, low tech)

AOL succeeded by defining its market. In 1992 it had two hundred thousand members. By 2001 it had thirty-two million members and had become a media giant. AOL distinguished itself by making online services easy for the masses to use. Many "techies" eschewed it, but people who didn't understand the intricacies of online communication were enticed to sign up. Of course, it didn't hurt that everywhere you turned there were disks announcing that you could get so many hours of AOL free. AOL also promoted a sense of community among its members and continues to expand that benefit today. (While AOL's original strategy of making Internet access easy and creating a sense of community was highly successful, it may have lost some of its attractiveness by now because customers are generally less intimidated by the Internet than they used to be.)

An owner of a radio station observed that 70 percent of the station's listeners were female, 65 percent owned homes, and 45 percent lived in households with income ranging from $25,000 to $49,000. This clear definition of his audience demographics gave him and his advertisers an understanding of their primary market.

"Nobody can sell anything they can't believe in."
—Dennis Eck, chief executive of Coles Myer,
the largest retail company in Australia

Why Do They Buy?

Typically, customers buy from two perspectives:

- *Value/quality/solutions:* These customers tend to make rational decisions and are concerned about budget, durability, and return on investment for their organizations.
- *Reliability/convenience/image:* These customers tend to make emotional decisions and are concerned about low buying risk, trust, and prestige for themselves.

The relative importance of each of these factors depends on the individual customer, but one thing is certain: customers must have some degree of excitement (emotion) about your product or service if you are going to make a sale. If they don't care, they won't buy. Logic, data, or a rational approach aren't always sufficient to change people's minds; they have to like what they hear. So even a proposal based on logic must have some degree of emotional appeal.

We tend to think of people who make decisions based on emotions as those people who show and express emotion. But everyone has emotions—it's just that some people don't show them as often or as openly. Some people base their emotions on logic, facts, or data as opposed to hunches, intuition, or trends, but they still have emotions. They may say something like, "The last vendor didn't meet our quality specifications" or "We count on you to get us everything you promised" or "Reliability is our first priority" or "We always come in under budget." All of these are expressions about what is important to these people or to their companies. They relate to resources, schedules, or deliverables. These people are expressing their expectations, priorities, and preferences. If you don't deliver, they will have a reaction. You can count on it.

The majority of business leaders are concerned about such things as quality, due dates, control, reliability, and flexibility. But many also focus on how much they feel they can trust the salesperson's competence, the reputation of the company the salesperson represents, whether people inside their organization will support their decision, and whether their decision will help or hurt their career.

Why is it important in sales to know how to appeal to people emotionally? Because no matter whom you are selling to, you have to get to their heart before you can get to their head. Before they are willing to nod their head in agreement, they have to be willing to admit that they like what they hear, are comfortable with the facts or data, and are willing to take the risk—however small it may be—to move ahead. If you neglect to connect with them at their gut level, you may not connect at all. Don't project your way of thinking onto the customer. Ask questions that allow you to determine their preferences; observe the way they like to work; then be consistent with those preferences, and you will find you have greater success making the sale.

Here is an example of how well this marketing strategy (identifying who your customers are and why they buy) can pay off. The largest car rental company isn't the one you probably think it is. As I write, the largest car rental company is one that focuses on supplying cars for people who are without their own cars temporarily (such as when their cars are being repaired). They developed and dominate a market that for the most part they don't share with the other car rental companies, because the other companies compete for business primarily at airports. The company is Enterprise. They get 95 percent of their business from local rentals.

A big part of Enterprise's market is supplying rental cars for people whose cars have been damaged in auto accidents. They work closely with auto insurers who make the reservation for the policyholder. Enterprise streamlined the rental process for insurers, bringing it online and making it user-friendly. The online system speeds up the process and lowers costs. As reported in *CIO* magazine, rentals from companies that use the online service have grown at two to three times the rates of companies that don't. Enterprise responded to the needs of these business customers, and in doing so kept itself positioned with its business partners in this market.

Another example is the insurance company USAA. USAA sells only to military officers and their dependents. It covers 95 percent of that market. Its formula, as described by chief executive Robert Herres in a 1996 *Fortune* article, is: "First, you decide who you want your customers to be. Then you decide what they need and want. Then you figure out which of those needs you can meet, and then you do that better than anyone else."*

Here's a quick way to find out what your customer or prospective customer sees as being most important in the buying decision. Use this approach once you know you are talking with the decision maker.

- Prepare a list of the criteria that should be used in making a decision to purchase your product or service.
- Don't put anything on the list that you can't do or don't do well.
- Ask the customer to tell you, in terms of importance to him or her, all the criteria that will bear on his or her purchase decision. To help you with this, see the suggested ideas in the following list:

Functionality	Service after the sale
Ease of use	Customized solutions
Reliability	Carefulness
Payment options	Uniqueness
Warranty	Ease of ordering
Attitude of employees	Ease of repair
Thoroughness	Durability
Variety of products	Delivery time
Convenience	Return policy
Ease of updating	Response time
Style	Prestige
Reputation	The salesperson
Money-back guarantee	Price or cost

Your list might include six items, for example. Once the customer has listed the items, you can then ask the customer to discuss why he or she considers each one to be important.

Seven Keys for Customer Relationships
- Where do your products have the best fit (now and in the future)?
- Which customers do you work best with?

---

* "Growing Your Company: Five Ways to Do It Right!" *Fortune* (November 25, 1996): 81.

- What kind of support does the customer want or expect?
- How much and what kind of communication does the customer want?
- What does the customer value most (in priority order)?
- How well are you performing in providing each aspect of what they expect?
- How well does your account team work to support the customer's needs?

"None of us sells anything that anyone needs."
—Bob Baker, who runs an off-road
course for Land Rover owners

Why Should They Buy from Your Company?

Michael E. Gerber, author of *Power Point Marketing* and *The E-Myth*, relates this question to brand recognition versus product acceptance. If the customer hasn't been sold on the idea of what you're selling, you must first gain product acceptance. Asking why customers buy can help you answer that question.

You've probably noticed that it is usually easier to get people to make a decision if they are already sold on an idea. Selling books to people who don't buy books or read much is a lot harder than selling books to someone who buys a lot of books. Even though at first you might want to sell to the people who haven't bought yet, you will use less time selling if you don't have to convince the prospect why the concept is good. So concentrating on people who are already sold on the product allows you to concentrate on selling the brand, yourself, or what you have to offer, and make sales *faster*.

I had the opportunity to work with PW Funding and interview their top producer, Dick Olrich, in getting ready for my program. (PW Funding was originally a part of Payne Webber. Since its inception in 1970, it has originated more than $3 billion of financing for multifamily housing. It is now a subsidiary of Related Capital.) Here's what Dick told me he does to provide value to his clients: "I convey to clients that

I am in the business of developing relationships, not one transaction. We give superior speed and service. We're not the most aggressive. We put forth a reasonable deal that works for the borrower and lender. We tend to screen conservatively. We deliver as promised."

When Dick joined the company ten years ago, it did very little repeat business. Now close to half of its business is repeat and a good deal of that is due to the process Dick developed to make sure he "takes away the headaches" of his customers, thus increasing the value of the services he provides to them.

> *"We have to build a brand that you don't have to keep explaining to your neighbors why your drive a Hyundai and not a Honda."*
> —Finbarr O'Neill, head of Hyundai U.S. sales

Typically, the most likely customers at the early stage are the small number who must have the latest technology or design. The mass market waits until the technology is proven, the design is accepted, and the product or service becomes very easy to use or is distributed through more convenient channels. This distinction may be important to you if you are selling a product that has not yet gained wide acceptance. While the lack of acceptance can make the sale more difficult, the lack of competition can make it easier.

When customers have bought from you, what was most important to them in making their decision to purchase? Understanding this can help you better market to *other* customers. From time to time, you'll want to ask your customers what was the most important reason they decided to do business with you.

To understand why new customers should buy from you, start by asking your *current* customers why they buy from you. Call or meet with three to five customers. A face-to-face meeting is best, but if you can't accomplish that, phone and E-mail can also work. Begin with these five questions:

- What benefits and results have I achieved for you? (Quantify, if possible.) Have I met, exceeded, or not met your expectations?
- What do you like best about my products or services? About working with me?

- What one, two, or three things could I do to serve you better?
- If you had a magic wand, what else would you wish for in the solutions that have been available from me or others? (What's missing?)
- What do you see as the most important trends affecting your purchase decisions in the future?

Note also that if you work at a medium-sized or large company, your company may conduct customer surveys. You might be able to gain some information from these surveys, or even piggyback onto them.

The relevance of these questions is that if you are selling to a strong market (a service tailored to those customers and with less competition), it is easier to sell. If there is not much difference between the next salesperson and you, it will be much more difficult to sell. (That's called a commodity market.)

With hundreds of cable channels, channels are evolving to target more and more specific audiences. Jack Trout, coauthor of *Positioning: The Battle for Your Mind*, a timeless marketing text, defines this as *positioning*. Positioning, he writes, is "simply concentrating on an idea—even a word—that defines the company in the minds of consumers."

Jack advises that when developing a position in the mind of the customer, it's best to keep it simple: "Just focus on one powerful attribute and drive it into the mind." The more involved and detailed the message is, the more confusing it will be and the less people will understand and remember it.

Wal-Mart chose to focus on low prices. When people think of Wal-Mart, they think of low prices. They advertise low or "falling" prices. This positioning became part of the Wal-Mart business model. Kmart, on the other hand, chose to advertise sale items in circulars that were costly to print and distribute and then incurred high costs to stock the sale items. The result was that these costs accounted for 10 percent of Kmart's operating expenses, compared to less than 1 percent for Wal-Mart.

The concept of positioning can apply to a company, a brand, or an individual. How do you go about positioning yourself in the minds of customers?

- Have a field of specialization and be the expert in it.
- Describe what you do for customers in a way that is easy to remember.

- Look for opportunities where there is a growing need for your expertise.
- Have the credentials to demonstrate your expertise.
- Get the word out about how you help your customers.

Positioning yourself as the person to call when someone needs an expert allows you to shift the demand curve so that you're sought after. This is a much better position to be in than having to convince people that they should give you a chance to speak with them. One caution: If you are sought after, don't become arrogant about it.

"When something doesn't sell well, I never say, 'Well, people don't understand it.' If people don't understand it, it doesn't belong in the store."
—Reed Krakoff, head designer, Coach, Inc.

How Do You Negotiate Price?

Differentiation determines why one product or service sells for more than another. People ask about price because it is a common denominator and easy to understand. But if people are only concerned with price, it is because they don't see the difference between one product and the next.

Price is an important part of most buying decisions, and it has become ever more important. When the economy is soft, price becomes a bigger component of the buying decision than when the economy is strong. With the advent of the Internet, high-speed communication, and data availability, it is now easier than ever to compare prices and features. There has also been an increasing emphasis on driving out costs from businesses as a way to keep prices low and competitive while making a satisfactory profit.

But think about it this way. Have you ever bought a product or service *solely* based on price? Didn't you also consider functionality, ease of use, style, durability, reliability, the reputation of the manufacturer or provider or vendor, delivery time, payment options, trustworthiness of the salesperson, and the guarantee or warranty?

Have you ever been offered a product or service that you wouldn't use even if it were free? Was it because it didn't suit your needs? Was it because it didn't do what you wanted it to do? Was it because you wouldn't have the time to use it or didn't like it? Was it because you thought it would be more work than it was worth? Was it because it didn't have the prestige you wanted?

Here's a quick example based on my preferences. I read a lot of business magazines. I subscribe to some. Some I receive free as a professional courtesy. But there are some that I refuse to take for free because it's going to take me time to look at it. Based on the value that I perceive I will derive from it, I choose to decline some of these free publications. (The quality of the publication isn't the issue; it's the relevance.) Now, there are others that I purchase. I like to get a good price for the subscription—I won't overpay. I'm sure you and your customers prefer to do likewise.

Can you think of situations in which you would buy a product or service where the price wasn't a deciding factor? Some possible examples could include:

- You needed it right away.
- Your life (or a family member's life) depended on it.
- Your job depended on it.
- Your relationship depended on it.
- There is no substitute.
- It gives you a strong competitive advantage (through advanced technology).
- Few others have one (it has prestige).

The number of times that one will buy something where price isn't an issue is minimal compared to the times when it is. In the vast majority of cases, the customer will factor it in. This is why you need to be sensitive to budget issues. If you ignore budget constraints, you will be blindsided.

If everything else is equal, people will go with the lowest price—but how often is everything else equal? And what can you do to ensure that it isn't by differentiating your product or service?

Recognize that if you need to justify a price, it is the *difference* in price, not the total price, that you must explain. And the difference in price can indeed be small when calculated over the useful life of the product or service.

Of course, while people may be willing to pay more for the same or a similar item for the sake of convenience or warranty, there is a limit to how much more they are willing to pay. Depending on the circumstances, 5 to 10 percent may be such a small difference that customers won't think twice about it, but 50 percent probably won't be. One client I worked with was told during a review after the company had lost a bid, "Your proposal was good, but it was hard to justify that much of a difference in price"—which, in their case, was 45 percent. Everyone wants the best price, but people are willing to work with a reasonable price in tradeoffs against other factors, such as delivery time or track record.

One additional viewpoint on price: price differentials on many items occur because of the way they are provided (or positioned). Food is a good example. You can buy the raw ingredients for a meal at the supermarket, or you can pay more for takeout, or pay even more at a gourmet restaurant for the very same ingredients. The price you are willing to pay depends on your tastes, convenience, ambience, and the service level you want and are willing to pay for.

I read an article in a restaurant magazine that described how to enhance the perceived value of ice cream as a dessert by the way it is presented—for example, the plate it is served on (have you noticed that the more upscale the restaurant, the larger the plates, whether or not the portions are?), the garnish, the name. (One client said, "Imagine how much of a following sushi would have if it were called raw, cold fish.") Enhanced service is one way to create a positive price differential, provided the customer sees the added service being of value.

For sales professionals, the question is, are there additional ways to enhance the customer's perception of the value of what you provide? Is there a different or better way to combine or package what you provide so that the customer will be willing to pay more for what he or she prefers? Can you offer more than one choice?

Many times, price is not the real objection. However, when price is the problem, it may be because the customer can't *afford* the product or service, though the customer may be reluctant to say that. Cash outlay may be the problem, which might be solved by financing or deferred payment.

So asking questions to determine whether price is the objection and whether the customer would like to hear about financing options can help resolve this issue. Showing potential cost savings or lost revenues are two other ways of helping to address this issue.

Getting customers to say why they don't want to purchase something is more than half the battle. Most people will not say. Why? They don't want a confrontation, they are embarrassed, or they don't want to discuss it or are afraid they'll end up arguing.

If you believe price is the objection, try to find out whether your belief is correct. Brian Tracy, CPAE, author of *The Psychology of Selling*, suggests asking, "If this item were free, would you take it?" If the answer is no, price really isn't the issue. (Again, you can probably think of something you wouldn't take even if it were free, which demonstrates this point.) This might be a time when you could illustrate the point with a story.

Not Right at Any Price

Have you ever bought something that you thought was a great bargain and that you could use, then took it home to your spouse and proudly showed off your bargain, only to get a response like, "Not in this house"? Was price the issue? When you acceded to your spouse's demands, what were you really selling? Respect for his or her wishes, perhaps? Peace, harmony? What would the real price have been if you persisted in bringing your treasure into the home?

Price Isn't the Same as Cost

Remember that price isn't the same as cost. Price is only the initial outlay. The total cost of ownership includes such things as maintenance, repairs, downtime, and servicing. How does your warranty compare to that of your competitors? What potential revenues might customers lose if they lose the use of the product? What are the consequences of downtime? Making your customer aware of cost savings that accrue from using your product or service can help you justify an initially higher price.

And while most want a reasonable price, they also want assurance that the service will work and that problems will not occur or will be fixed quickly if they do occur.

Have you ever bought something that saved a little money initially but eventually ended up costing much more? How much did you save on the initial purchase? How much more did it cost you later? If it was a lot of money, isn't it something you would rather not repeat? Can you recall the emotion you felt when you incurred the additional cost?

Most people—your customers included—can think of their own examples if you asked them the same question. I can think of a painful one: I "saved" $25, but it cost me $7,500. My wife and I were selling our home, which had a well that supplied our water. The buyer was going to have the water tested, but I wanted to make sure that it would pass inspection, so I decided to have the well inspected myself so I could get any problems corrected, even though I had never noticed any problem with the water. I called the water testing company, which said two tests were available: I could bring a sample of water to them in a sterile container and they would test it for $25, or they could come out and take the sample for $60. I said I thought the $25 test would be good. The representative said that the results wouldn't be certified because they couldn't be sure where the sample came from, but I said that would be satisfactory because the buyers were going to do their own test. That turned out to be a false savings.

The sample showed no problems in the well. The day before the closing, the buyer's attorney's office called and asked about the water report. I had forgotten that there was no follow-up test. So someone came out and took a sample. I took the sample from the sterilized faucet in the kitchen, but he took it from the hot water heater in the basement, a damp environment where it would be more difficult to get a clean sample. I tend to believe that he did not sterilize the faucet well. The next morning, just hours before we were supposed to close, we learned that the sample had failed the test. To close, we had to place $7,500 into escrow to cover the cost of a new well, if one was needed—and of course, with the buyer in control, they ended up putting in a new well. We could have not closed, but at that point we felt that wasn't a viable option. To this day, I believe that if I had the fellow come out to take the sample and if he had done it properly, the well would have passed.

So the moral of the story is that while you sometimes save a little on a purchase, it can cost you a lot. Most of us can think of a time when we saved a little and spent a lot. Your prospective customers can probably also think of an example, which is a good way to illustrate that cost can be much more than the price. (By the way, besides the $7,500, we had the emotional uncertainty and stress to deal with, which doesn't have a pricetag.)

Asking the prospective customer to answer this question is one of the most important ways of negating the issue of price. You have an advantage when total cost is considered along with all the other results you get for your customers.

Customers, whether they are consumers or businesses, have become more price sensitive. We need only look at the popularity of buying clubs, superstores, and discount outlets for proof of this. Businesses are streamlining and looking for ways to cut costs. Cost is an issue we cannot ignore. It's therefore more important than ever to not be considered just a commodity, no different from the next product or service, but to stand out for reasons important to customers.

Unfortunately, too many salespeople and too many companies react to the price issue by just cutting price. They condition the customer to expect more and continuing price cuts, resulting in price-conscious and fickle customers who have little, if any, reason to stay with a company because they know someone will come along with a lower price.

Changing the Price Affects How Many Units Are Sold

Why is it that certain products or services must compete more on price than others? In part, it is because they are not distinguished well from those other products or services. But it also may be due to the maturity of the product or service in the marketplace. It is a bit of theory, but the following explanation will put a framework around some of the pricing issues you face and the customer responses you've seen.

When products or services are new and address a problem that customers are anxious to solve, they command a premium price; they tend to be in short supply, and demand outpaces supply. Once a product gains acceptance, it also encourages competitors. Those competitors provide alternatives. Those alternatives change what is called the *elasticity of demand*. The elasticity of demand describes what happens when a supplier changes the price for a product. If there is a high elasticity of demand, when the supplier changes the price—even a small amount—it greatly affects the demand. If there is a low elasticity of demand, when the supplier changes the price it hardly affects the demand. Of course, suppliers like products with a low elasticity of demand.

Figure 4 below illustrates these differences between two products, A and B. When the price for product A is increased, demand goes down just a little. People continue to buy the product, but in slightly smaller quantities. So raising the price would probably result in more revenue. When the price for product B is increased, the demand drops sharply. Product B has a higher elasticity of demand than product A. The supplier of product A could conceivably raise the price and make more money, because the cost of the product would probably stay pretty much the same. The supplier of product B, while making more money per unit, may make much less money in total because many fewer units will be sold.

The elasticity of demand changes over time, depending on the market and how distinct the product or service is. More mature products or services have a higher elasticity of demand (reflective more of a commodity), which means that the way the product or service is delivered can affect the price. If the market is growing and demand can't be as easily satisfied, then prices tend to remain strong. If the market is static or shrinking, supply will tend to exceed demand, and prices will soften.

A good rule of thumb is that the lower the price, the more people will buy. Exceptions are those items that are valued because they are higher priced. Prestige brands fall into this category. There is an element of exclusivity about the brand because not everyone can afford it, so if the price were significantly lower fewer people might purchase it. The other extreme is when the price is so low that it makes people wonder whether there is something wrong with the product. But there aren't

Figure 4

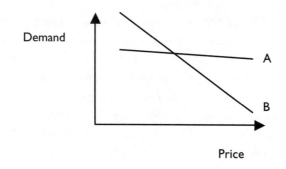

too many exceptions to the rule of thumb: the lower the price, the more people will buy.

Something else to keep in mind is that sometimes you are competing not against someone who sells the same thing, but someone who is competing for your customer's dollars. Electronic equipment sales were strong until car companies offered zero-percent financing. Consumers chose to buy cars instead of electronics. When the economy is slow, people may not take exotic vacations; they may go out to the movies or restaurants more often.

What does this mean for you as a sales professional? It means that if you started out selling a unique product with few competitors, but now find yourself facing more competitors and more price competition, you will encounter more price sensitivity. You will need to differentiate yourself in the marketplace so that customers see you as an important part of their purchase of your product or service.

You're going to need to exert care when it comes to pricing. What worked early in the product's life cycle won't necessarily work later. What works when a market segment is strong won't work when it's shrinking. One defense contractor, commenting on the change in the defense budget, said, "Cost is of the essence to the customers, because they don't have the budget they used to."

As a sales professional, you don't design the product or service you sell, but you can affect the way you sell it and the value you add to it.

Adding a level of service will allow you to compete more effectively against those who have poor service.

I've spent a lot of time discussing the issue of price because it is a critical factor in buying decisions. Price is the easiest way to judge a product because it is easy to understand. But price needs to be placed in context. Do what you can to position yourself so you aren't competing solely on price. At the same time, don't ignore the issue. Look for ways to enhance your perceived value. Look for ways to deliver higher value to customers. Do it while lowering their costs, which adds to their bottom line, and they will continue to buy from you.

The Core of Law 2: Decide on Your Market

Be clear about who your customers are, what you do for them, the value you promise to deliver, why they should buy from you at what price level, and the results they derive.

DEVELOP CUSTOMER EXPERTISE IN YOUR SELECTED MARKET

Become a resource, someone your customers know they can count on. Being a resource means being helpful and supportive. How can you become a resource for your customers? Here are five ideas to consider:

- Walk in the customer's shoes.
- Educate your customer.
- Sell solutions at the highest level.
- Be easy to do business with.
- Help the customer make a decision.

Walk in the Customer's Shoes

"Walking in the customer's shoes" means understanding your customer's business and the issues that are critical to their success. Simply put, you ask yourself questions like, What might this person be experiencing? What are the factors critical to their success? Many people understand this concept, but not everyone sees its importance or practices it regularly. Yet it is absolutely key to truly serving the customer well.

I know of one salesperson who put this concept in action. He was attempting to get his foot in the door with a large fast-food franchiser. Because he didn't have a contact in the prospective company, he decided to find out firsthand the business issues this company was facing by taking a part-time weekend job for a short time at one of its outlets. Then he followed up with a letter that discussed the issues he observed based on his firsthand experience. The customer was impressed with his thoroughness.

How can you walk in the customer's shoes? Asking good questions and listening are the first steps, of course. Here are other ideas you can use, with the customer's permission:

- Conduct in-depth interviews of their top performers.
- Spend at least a half day observing their work operation.
- Spend at least a half day working in their operation.
- Sit in on one of their meetings and observe.
- Listen to their executives.
- Talk with their customers.
- Work on a project team in their operation.
- Experience the best (increased earnings) and worst (cutbacks) of their work.

Item 2 on this list, spending time observing their work operation, can provide critical data. It will allow you to understand how your customer really uses your product or service (or their current supplier) or how they have adapted it to suit their needs. You may see how they overcome little inconveniences or work around less than perfect solutions. You may get to talk with some of their operational people and hear their opinions. Observing firsthand the customer's operation will provide unique insights that you can't get elsewhere. This will give you a competitive advantage that will be more than worth the time you invest.

Here is an example I experienced. I have done hundreds of presentations at meeting facilities in the U.S. and Canada. In all that time, never have any facility staff approached me to say, "I would like to understand what you have to do to get ready." Sometimes (and it doesn't happen as often as it should) someone will stop by just to ensure that everything is set up according to what was ordered and is satisfactory. But until they observe firsthand what I do, they cannot really understand the importance of the many details that have to be attended to in preparation for the meeting I'm conducting (such as making sure that there is sufficient room between the chairs, that the air-conditioning or heating is working properly, that electrical wires have been taped down, or that there is no noise coming into the room from an adjoining room). They wouldn't have to do what I do—they could just stay for part of the presentation and observe, or even just ask. They understand what they need to do from *their* point of view (get the coffee in, get the chairs set up, and so on), and they usually do it well. But having an understanding from my point of view would result in even greater customer satisfaction.

All of us have been told at some point that we could improve certain areas of performance. Even though we may have recognized the advice as accurate and well intended, we may have been reluctant to go to the trouble to address the weakness. The advice interfered with our plans, created a problem, required us to do some things differently—to change. Being aware of the human tendency to resist suggestions for improvement can help us heed good advice so we can change what we're doing before our weaknesses result in negative consequences.

What have you done, what do you do, or what *could* you do as a professional to walk in *your* customer's shoes?

Educate Your Customers

If customers don't understand a product, they won't buy it. Customers become educated through experience. Make it your goal to educate your customers so they can better understand the products or services you offer. Of course, when they are more educated they become more sophisticated and are more likely to know better what they want or don't want, what it will take to get it, and how much it should cost. They are also more likely to negotiate when they are educated, but this can become a selling advantage if you can uniquely meet their needs. Of course, many customers educate *themselves*.

It is often advantageous for companies to establish partnerships with other companies that have complementary services and that don't compete. By working together, they produce solutions that are easier and less costly for customers. But in order to get the backing of the partner, salespeople have to educate the partner about the product or services just as they would educate an end user: What is it? What does it do? Why would it be advantageous for them? Demonstrations, training, or onsite visits are effective ways of doing this.

The goal is typically to provide an integrated solution to the end user. Salespeople may have to sell people in the partner organization on the idea and show them the sales potential. They may have to work to get approval. Then they may need to take it out to their customers. By working this way, companies produce "turnkey" solutions that the customer can use without having to find the expertise to bring together the components. This isn't uncommon, for example, in situations that require sophisticated hardware and software to work together or in which a variety of older systems must work together when a new component is installed.

When Starbucks was just beginning to develop into a national presence, one of the challenges the company faced was helping consumers understand the difference between the premium coffees it served and the coffees that most Americans were used to drinking. After all, why would Americans want to pay extra for something if they didn't think it was worth it? Starbucks demonstrated the advantages of its coffee by helping people to understand that there are different types of coffee and letting the taste of the product speak for itself. The book by Starbucks chairman and CEO Howard Schultz, *Pour Your Heart Into It*, among other things, provided an opportunity to educate an ever-expanding market about coffee.

Can a car insurance company educate its customers about how to lower their insurance costs? Mine does by providing a table that lists the injury, collision, and theft records for all cars. It helps me to understand the insurance costs for cars I am considering purchasing.

Can you educate customers too well? Possibly. But the more likely situation is that your efforts to educate the customer will generate business and loyalty.

American Express offers to educate the employees of companies on a range of financial topics—from financial planning to diversification and retirement planning to education funding and estate planning—

with a program free of specific product promotions. According to information provided on their website, American Express Financial Education and Planning Services sought the opinions of executives, human resource managers and employees from 80 different companies before designing their educational and planning programs. The key, they say, is that retirement has changed, that individuals need to be more self-reliant and better prepared. With that as a backdrop, they suggest that employees want more financial education at work and promise to deliver bottom-line results when employees have better financial information and make more informed decisions about their benefits, for example. Since it's clear that retirement has indeed changed, the promise of free comprehensive financial education would be attractive to companies and their employees. One would imagine that such an entrée would be very helpful to American Express salespeople, provided the program provides value and delivers on its promise of an objective, product-free educational program.

Sell Solutions at the Highest Level

Table 1 illustrates another way of looking at how to solve customer problems. Sales take place at different levels. Some sales require what I call the *clerk approach*. If I'm buying a toothbrush and the store clerk started asking about how often and how long I brush, I'd run. I just need a toothbrush. Some sales require the *salesperson approach*. If I'm buying a computer, I need to buy one that will help me with the kind of work I do. Knowing the number of gigahertz and gigabytes doesn't help me much, except to assure me that it's big and fast. If I am making strategic decisions about my business, I want someone who understands it in their area of expertise better than I do—someone who takes a *consultant approach*. Unfortunately, too many salespeople take the clerk approach when they should be taking the salesperson approach. Just think about your own experience in buying cars, computers, or other moderately priced equipment. When business issues are involved and you want to establish a longer-term relationship with the customer, a consultant approach will help you accomplish that.

Table 1 Three Ways to Sell

Clerk	Salesperson	Consultant
Sells features	Sells needs/benefits	Sells system solutions
Takes the order	Asks for the order	Creates the order
Wants to make the sale	Wants the next sale	Wants the relationship
Contact is purchasing department	Contact is department head	Contact is executive
Customer concern is price	Customer concern is performance	Customer concern is profit

A *Wall Street Journal* report on a survey of people shopping for consumer electronics showed that shoppers don't rely heavily on store employees for information. Of those who were asked where they got information about shopping for consumer electronics, many more said they got information from friends or relatives or ads than from the store staff.

Generally, the higher the level of sales contact, the less concern there is with price. The higher up the sale is made, the greater is the authority in making the decision. A purchasing agent who has limited authority may see a $40,000 purchase as a big risk that requires research and the involvement of others and will be less concerned about how long it takes to make a decision. An executive who has broad budget authority and who can move money from one budget item to another or change the budget, if necessary, may not see a $40,000 investment as a big deal when viewed against the payoff from that investment and will want to move as quickly as possible once convinced about the return on investment.

Keep this in mind: each level has its own point of concern. Depending on which level you are selling to, you are going to see that concern reflected by the person you are dealing with.

- For the purchasing agent, it tends to be *price*.
- For the user, it tends to be *performance*.
- For the executive, it tends to be *profit*.

Your best course of action is to be prepared to sell at all three levels: show how your solution will produce profits at the level of performance the users require at a competitive price.

At what level in your customer's organization are you selling now? At what level do you want to be selling, and why? What will help you sell to that level?

Be Easy to Do Business With

One of the greatest challenges in working with people is having consistent behavior with customers. A customer can encounter one employee one day and a different person the next. Their styles can be very different. Even encounters with the same person don't always produce the same interaction. Our moods depend on many things, some of which relate to personal factors. Because business involves humans, behaving in a consistent way in terms of professionalism, attitude, knowledge, and skills can be challenging. The key is customer expectations. If they come to expect a certain response to their needs, and less is provided, they may be disappointed, surprised, or angry. The relationship will be diminished. Almost more than the level of response, *customers value consistency*. If I go to a restaurant that consistently offers a moderate level of service, I know what I can expect. I can *rely* on it. But to have them attempt to deliver a higher level of service, only to succeed sometimes and fail others, is worse than not attempting to do it at all.

If you can deliver consistent service, you can capitalize on it as a selling advantage. If you can exceed the minimum expectations and do things that are unexpected but welcomed by customers, so much the better. But too many providers ruin their opportunities for ongoing customer relationships by being unreliable and inconsistent.

In his book *Leadership Is an Art*, Max DePree describes how he put the principle "the customer is always right" into practice in his company. If the customer wanted something, his employees' reaction would be "What can we do to get them what they want?" not "Our policy [or our computer, or my authority, and so on] won't permit me to do that." If the customer wanted billing on a certain date and in a certain format, even if the company's computer was not normally set up to do it, they found a way to make it happen. If the customer asked for what seemed like the impossible, they worked creatively to make it possible.

DePree defined the real meaning of "the customer is always right" and made it easy to do business with his company. "The customer is always right" doesn't mean that customers may not be misinformed or do things that are wrong. It simply means that if you listen to the customer's request, you may find a way to satisfy it. It is a matter of perspective: looking for ways to satisfy the customer's request rather than finding reasons why you can't.

How consistent are you at delivering what customers expect? How do you know? How easy is it to do business with you or your company? How do you know? There's only one way to find out: ask.

More than being a resource, you can become a partner with your customers. You are a partner when customers can't do without you. You are a partner when you are aligned with the customers' goals, making sure that you know those goals thoroughly and that whatever you do supports their ability to achieve those goals. When you are a partner with the customer, you are privy to information that isn't available to everyone.

Help the Customer Make a Decision

If you have a product or service that provides worthwhile benefits, you have an obligation to present it to customers and help them decide whether it is the right solution for them. If you don't bring the product or service to the attention of a customer who could use it, he or she will have to tolerate problems they could solve.

Have you ever been approached by a salesperson with a product you liked, and then not been asked to buy? One survey found that only one in five customers would offer to buy when they weren't asked. There are times when salespeople don't ask for the sale, hoping the customer will offer to purchase the product or service.

When you begin, ask permission to ask for the sale later. You might say something along the lines of "When we are finished, if I can meet your needs, would you be comfortable with my suggesting that we move ahead with this purchase?" What I don't suggest you do is to use one of the standard clichés that salespeople have been taught and customers have gotten tired of hearing, such as "Would Monday or

Wednesday be better for a delivery?" In my opinion, those clichés work against you.

Why is it that some salespeople don't ask for a decision? They'd prefer not to hear no. But if you have a good product, one you believe in, you're almost obliged to find out whether it will help the customer and, if it will, to get the customer comfortable making a purchase decision. If you don't and the customer never gets the benefits of the product or service, then you have not been of service to you or your company. That's what sales leaders do.

A salesperson for a water purification company came to my home one day. He had a simple demonstration that was persuasive. He showed, by dropping chemicals into my tap water, that there was more chlorine in the tap water than in my swimming pool. It was convincing. But I wanted to see whether he would ask me for the sale. We talked and talked, but he never asked me to buy.

Five Nonthreatening, Easy Ways to Ask for the Sale

- I really want to earn your business. What would help me do that?
- How does what we've discussed so far match with what you were looking for?
- What other information would you need to make a decision?
- What would your reasons be for deciding to purchase this?
- Would you be comfortable recommending this as the best solution? (This is the type of question you'll want to ask if the person you are working with must represent your proposal to other decision makers, such as a committee.)

These questions will help you move toward the sale or discover that there isn't a match. Just as important as the questions is the way they are asked. A caring, sincere tone of voice will come across as less confrontational.

Does the Customer Really Know What He or She Wants?

In sales, we say we need to give customers what they want. But if you've been in sales for any length of time I'm sure you have encountered customers who didn't seem to know what they wanted. It may not happen often, but when it does it is disruptive and time consuming. It's best to red-flag the prospects that might be problematic early on and avoid or at least minimize a time commitment with them. Clearly, you would be much better off investing your time with the ideal customers to realize a worthwhile payoff.

Most customers know what they want. Even if they only know what they *don't* want, at least you can go through a process of elimination to construct options. But when customers can't articulate what they are looking for, when they change their minds, or when they seem to continually find little things that eliminate one proposal after another, you are probably going to find that coming to a resolution either takes too much of your time or is not possible. You end up feeling exasperated. You start to wonder how much more time you should sink into winning the business, but are reluctant to cut your losses because of what you've invested already. The customer keeps dangling the carrot and you keep going after it.

Not all customers are created equal. You need to be sure you understand the customer well enough to be able to make an informed decision about how much time you should invest in him or her.

What are the signs that can help you decide whether to go ahead and, if you do, how much time or money to invest in attempting to win the sale? Ask yourself questions like these:

- What is the potential size of the sale?
- How many people are bidding on the work?
- Do I have a special advantage?
- What does a cost-benefit assessment show?
- What are the best- and worst-case scenarios?
- Is there a way to more efficiently put together a proposal for promising prospects that would allow me to balance the cost-benefit trade-offs?

The more desperate you are to win the business, the more likely you are to ignore telltale signs that the customer will be a time drain, and the longer it will take you to realize it. Table 2 will help put parameters around the issues that you must confront in working with different

Table 2 Customer Types

Customer Type	Ideal	Promising	Difficult
Buying criteria	Value-based, clear, a good match with your offerings	Basic, not sophisticated, workable	Subject to change, uncertain, price focused
Business issues	Pressing and relevant	Emerging	Crisis prone
Decision	Quick	Reasonable	Prolonged
Budget	Available now	Later	Questionable
Decision authority	One or two people at most	Consensus/committee	Not formalized or uncertain
Customer qualities	Knowledgeable, open to new ideas, honest, moves quickly to finalize agreement, accommodates your needs	New in job or field, just forming opinions, welcomes suggestions, relies on colleagues	Slow response, new boss, not flexible, always wants multiple vendor submissions, procrastinator, price shopper
What to do	Pursue (work toward an agreement)	Develop (keep in touch with)	Avoid (or make only one standard offer)

FIVE DOS AND FIVE DON'TS OF SELLING

Do
- Understand the customer's real buying motivations
- Ask questions and listen
- Have integrity
- Be prepared
- Ask for and assume the order (with a good solution)

Don't
- Push your own agenda
- Do most of the talking
- Ignore the details
- Leave anything to chance
- Forget to thank the customer, ask for feedback, and suggest referrals

---

types of customers. While there are no exact rules, the table provides a framework for thinking about and recognizing the type of customer situation you have and doing it early enough to take advantage of it or to cut your losses. Some customers may have some of the qualities from different columns, so the categorization of the customer as *ideal, promising,* or *difficult* may be blurred—but you can still gain a better understanding about what to do by thinking about it this way than not thinking about it at all.

The Core of Law 3: Develop Customer Expertise in Your Selected Market

Seek out ideal customers and sell solutions at the highest customer level by being an expert in your product and your customer's industry and business.

BUILD RELATIONSHIPS FOR REPEAT BUSINESS

Long-term relationships are based on trust and integrity. Integrity is doing the right thing. Trust is established by honesty, competency, consistency, and follow-through.

Time after time, salespeople describe their industry to me as "a relationship business," reflecting their belief that to cultivate repeat business, salespeople must develop relationships. As we said when we started, customers buy from those they trust. If they are misled, they take the solemn vow, "I will never buy from that company again." So developing and protecting the relationship you have with your customers becomes paramount to your ability to grow your business.

Salespeople also say that this is a people business, which it is. While sales depend on products or services and the companies that supply them, it's people who make decisions about whether to buy. Outstanding salespeople have a balance between their technical and people skills. Salespeople who are too technical may lose business when people can't relate to them. Salespeople who are too focused on the relationship may lose business to salespeople who are able to put together a good technical solution.

Relationships in this context are all about trust. Can your customer trust you to deliver what you've promised, when you've promised it, at the price you've promised, and to stand behind it with service when needed? If you were to ask your customers, you would probably find that most of them have been burned at some time in their careers by someone who oversold them. They don't want it to happen again. So when they find a trustworthy supplier, they value that relationship.

Too many salespeople work on a transactional basis. They are out to make the sale, regardless of whether it will lead to additional business. They won't turn down business that they legitimately should. They may overpromise and underdeliver. They may be product peddlers instead of problem solvers. They have no meaningful business relationship with the customer beyond getting paid for that one transaction. It's an expensive way to do business.

The relationship is about trust in how you and your company perform. Always keep in mind that it is your consistent delivery of solutions to your customers' problems that will keep them coming back.

Three Common Mistakes Salespeople Make

How do salespeople run into difficulties with customers? *Sales and Marketing Management* magazine in its February 2000 issue featured interviews with buyers responsible for billions of dollars in purchases. Their insights reflected these areas of concerns:

- They stay with their own agenda instead of trying to understand the customer's. Salespeople who do this often don't listen to what customers have to say or ask what they want. (They don't use a consultative approach.)
- They don't plan well, which often means that they will not have well-thought-out call objectives.
- They don't add value to the sale, either because they don't have solid product knowledge or they don't understand the customer's business, industry, or issues.

What Do Customers Value in a Salesperson?

In interviews I've done with customers of my clients, the following qualities emerged as those that customers value in a salesperson:

- Credibility—honors commitments
- Attitude—willing to go the extra mile
- Communication—keeps customers informed
- Thorough product knowledge
- Understands customer needs
- Support—never lets customers down

Credibility means that you can be trusted to do what you say you will do. The right *attitude* makes you willing to go to bat for customers, taking every step possible to get them what they need and always maintaining a can-do, positive outlook. *Communication* means that you keep customers informed about price or product changes and status of orders, and that you respond quickly to phone calls. *Thorough product knowledge* is self-explanatory, but you'd be surprised at how it can set you apart. *Understanding customer needs* may mean looking beyond the buyer to the user and even to their customers. *Support* is never taking the customer for granted, never letting your guard down.

When you work with your customers within this set of responsibilities, they recognize, respond to, and reward it. You may have noticed that the items listed form the acronym CACTUS. A cactus is a tough, prickly plant that can take the heat. This image is an appropriate reminder of the toughness needed to succeed in sales.

Customer Relationships Defined

Sales are built on relationships. But what does a business relationship look like? How is it different from a personal relationship? Can you mix the two? Should you?

Customers are interested in business relationships because they expect certain results from that relationship. What they want varies depending on the customer, but some common themes emerge.

All people enter into relationships because they expect to get something from them. In personal relationships, we look for love, compassion, support, understanding, companionship, fun, immortality, and strengths we don't have. Business relationships are different. Business-people typically want predictable and consistent performance, outcomes, and support that helps them succeed in their careers. They usually want to work with people who make their work easier. They often have their own customers to satisfy. They may want low-risk solutions, they may want to keep a low profile, or they may want innovation. But you can see the clear distinctions between personal and business relationships. When you confuse a business relationship with a personal relationship, you can end up losing the business relationship.

During a discussion in one of my sales programs, one executive related how he and his company had a strong relationship with one of their largest customers. They had such a strong relationship that when the sales executive went to the customer's town, they went out to dinner together and he stayed at the customer's home. It had been this way for a long time. But all of a sudden, he got a call from the customer saying he was switching his business to a competitor. You can imagine how shocked and chagrined the executive was.

He acknowledged that he had mistaken the personal relationship for a business one, and in the process ended up not being aware that a competitor had even approached the customer. The customer, quite naturally, also saw the relationship as a personal one. He didn't place a great deal of value on it from a business point of view, which actually was consistent with what he saw from the supplier.

Building Customer Relationships Is a Critical Part of Selling

I surveyed sales professionals at a national sales meeting about their experience in developing and maintaining relationships with customers. Here is a compiled and edited summary of their responses.

What are the benefits of having a productive business relationship with the customer?

- They think of you right away when they need help or solutions. They more easily share long-term business issues, research and development initiatives, and access to future business plans. They will give you first shot at new business.

- You get mutual problem solving and mutual growth in profitability. You get repeat business. You gain the ability to introduce new products and increase business. You know the internal structure and practices of a company so you can better meet their current needs and anticipate future ones. You can develop new opportunities with decision makers in other divisions.
- Communication is much better. They give you a heads-up on problems and will work with you to resolve them. You are more aware of what's happening with the customer and the customer's organization. You get answers when you need them. You get access to people. You get the truth, including honest feedback on pricing.
- It's more difficult to get displaced by price. The customer may offer information on competitive situations. You get a second chance. In a tie, you win. You're able to use the customer for a testimonial and referral to similar customers.
- Time is used much more productively. Less time is involved in routine business transactions. Both organizations share the benefits of increased sales volume.

What do you do to help build strong relationships with your customers?

- Be honest about what you can and cannot do. Always keep your commitments. Look for mutually beneficial solutions and outcomes. Follow through on what you say you'll do.
- Make their jobs easier. Make them more productive. Educate, plan, and then execute together.
- Always return calls promptly. Ask about call frequency. Always respond to their request even if the answer is negative.
- Bring them customers and help them make more money. Support them with ideas, targets, and joint calls.
- Provide the best possible support after the sale. Be accessible. Get them technical support when they need it.
- Be available, be trustworthy, and show interest and understanding.
- Understand their objectives and help them to achieve them.

- Gain understanding of their business process and their products.
- Keep up with industry trends.
- Solve their problems by thinking "out of the box."
- Communicate with all levels in the company.
- Make their concerns your concerns. Put a high priority on addressing them.
- Know your products and their applications.
- Communicate about new products and offer assistance and training for them.
- Schedule planned visits with specific purposes and outcomes in mind. Use an agenda.
- Get to know the engineering, planning, financial, and administrative people in the account.
- Listen, listen, listen. Learn their business and treat every issue with concern.
- Convince the customer that you want to work to solve their problems.
- Do what you say and follow up until you are absolutely sure everything has been handled to their satisfaction. Ask them how satisfied they are with you, your company, and its products or services. Ask them for a forthright assessment of what you can do to improve. Let them know they can count on you to go to bat for them any time.

What have you found you need to avoid in maintaining good relationships?

- Don't get caught up in internal politics. Don't get involved in rumors, gossip, or complaints. Never play he said, she said. Avoid internal power plays. (You'll end up on the wrong side at some point.) Don't leave people out of the loop, either intentionally or unintentionally.
- Don't knock your competition. (This includes warning the customer about a competitor's financial problems.) Also avoid comparing or discussing the *customer's* competition.
- Make sure you really can fix their needs with your product applications. Be cautious of untested solutions.

- Don't be pushy or become complacent about the customer, the relationship, or your performance.
- Let the customers determine how personal they want the relationship to be. Never waste their time. Don't allow a personal relationship to interfere with business decisions.
- Identify problem areas and then don't go there: religion, politics, call waiting, answering the phone during customer meetings. Avoid giving advice on personal issues. Don't offer an opinion if it wasn't asked for. Avoid things that are too personal.
- Be careful of the humor and language you use.
- Avoid negativity of any kind toward anyone or anything. Avoid the appearance of conflicts of interest and avoid putting customers in such a position.
- Avoid anything illegal or illicit.
- Avoid negative comments on business surroundings.
- Avoid revisiting problems that have been solved.
- Don't put down the people who work in your company or their company.
- Take responsibility for problems.

Building strong customer relationships helps build loyalty. Building relationships allows you to partner with and be integrated into the customer's company. You're not considered just another salesperson pushing product. You and your customer can have a sense of trust about your relationship. Never take the relationship for granted—as soon as you do, you'll start to lose the trust that you worked so hard to gain.

Marriott International is a leader. Its salespeople are recognized as being among the best in the hospitality industry. How do they do it? John Marriott, executive vice president of lodging for Marriott International (which includes sales and marketing), said, "At Marriott, our salespeople are highly regarded because they are knowledgeable about their customers and spend as much time listening as they do selling. They welcome feedback and always follow up on concerns and issues."

When asked what advice he would pass along to new and experienced salespeople who wanted to truly be successful, he responded as follows:

To be successful in sales, you must spend time building relationships with your customers and learning as much about them and their business as possible. This is best accomplished by getting out of the office and meeting the customer face to face, not sitting back waiting for the phone to ring. From the junior salesperson to the CEO, it is critical that every salesperson establish solid relationships and true understanding of the wants and needs of his or her customers. Use every interaction as an opportunity to strengthen your relationship.

Effective salespeople are also highly confident. They know what they are talking about. I recommend that any salesperson going after a piece of business spend time learning about their customer's company and looking for ways to provide service and value that is relevant to their needs. Your knowledge, understanding, and interest will be highly appreciated and will play a key role in your ability to complete a sale. As you learn about your customer's business and develop relationships within the organization, you'll be viewed as an active partner and someone who is helping the company succeed.

For the more experienced salesperson, John concluded by stressing the importance of staying close to customers: "Don't take them for granted. This is just what your competition is waiting for—an opportunity to call on a customer that you have failed to visit or contact. It is also important to stay current. Their business will grow and change along with what they expect from you. By constantly staying focused on your customer's wants and needs, you will earn their trust and respect and establish a solid relationship that will be profitable for everyone."

It's clear from John Marriott's comments and from all of the other points discussed in this section that maintaining a business relationship is a critical priority. The following three recommendations can help you make it work.

- *Protect the trust you have developed in the relationship.* Selling something that can't be delivered the way the customer expects is a sure way to lose trust. Walking away from the sale if there isn't a match is a sure way to develop trust. People do not like being dependent on others. When they trust someone, that's what happens. Trust is fragile. If it is lost, it is not easily won back. It is possible to win people back under those circumstances if you act quickly, but it's best never to lose your customer's trust.

- *Make the time to listen and attend to the customer's concerns and needs.* At one of my programs, attendees had to come up to the second level on the escalator to get to the room. As they came off the escalator, it wasn't clear which direction they needed to go. My assistant asked someone from the conference staff to set up a sign to show people which way to go. His response was, "I don't have time for that." I know helping us was not on his agenda for that morning. But if he didn't have time for the customers, what did he have time for? What was most important? Salespeople who find their customers' concerns or questions to be a bother will find that customers will stop bothering them.

- *Recognize that it all depends on your knowledge, attitude, and resolve.* Winning a sale is not something that takes place at the end of a sale. It should be a natural progression from the beginning of the interaction. You can be more successful when you combine up-to-date industry and customer knowledge with the right attitude, and then back it with resolve. Resolve means deciding ahead of time not to quit, no matter what, bouncing back from setbacks and putting your knowledge to use to be better tomorrow than today.

An Integrated Solution

"Wow!" That's how fans respond to Reliant Stadium, home to the Houston Texans football franchise. According to Steve Patterson, senior vice president and chief development officer for the Texans, once people get to the building they are awed. "It's been an overwhelmingly positive response, whether it's the open-air stadium keeping fans cool with the air control systems, the media and their access to state-of-the-art communications, or the safety and security of the facility. We tried to make this building the best it could be in every aspect, and it turned out that way."

Patterson credits much of this success to the company that won the bid and became his "technology partner," Siemens. Siemens is a network encompassing more than 426,000 people in 193 countries. It provides customers with a "business portfolio" of solutions in the fields of information and communications, automation and control, power, lighting, transportation, and medical. But rather than send in representatives from each of its divisions to sell individual products and services as independent units, the company approached Reliant Stadium as one organization with an integrated solution across its multiple product lines. The integrated solution that the Siemens sales team developed for Reliant Stadium included all of its technologies from throughout its vast organization. Moreover, Siemens proposed that it be the infrastructure general contractor on the project, which would lead to further cost savings during construction. This was an innovative sales approach developed and led by the sales team, starting with its vision for the stadium, which came from understanding the customer's business needs.

Understanding the Customer

Owen Arkison, one of the Siemens sales executives who oversaw this sale, said: "The Siemens sales team developed a vision for how its systems could save money and enhance revenue for the stadium's owner and tenants. The sales team did this by seeking to understand not just the customers' technical needs, which you'd expect, but by also understanding the customers' businesses and their individual needs. The various Siemens companies worked together to present a plan for an integrated solution, one that would not only save money, but that would also enhance the complex's ability to deliver the best sporting experience possible."

The sales team went through a detailed process over a span of more than a year to understand the unique business situation and each of the stakeholders' individual needs. It was a special situation because there is one owner of the facility (the county) and two tenants (the Houston Texans and RODEOHOUSTON, the world's largest rodeo), each with distinctly different needs. In trying to understand their needs, Arkison said the question became, "How can we help them do their business and generate income?" In the case of the Texans, for example, an important source of income is suite sales. The county, on the other hand, wanted a high-tech facility that would operate at a reasonable cost and that would bring in convention and other entertainment business.

Creating Value Through Vision

Siemens's vision for the project was to provide a state-of-the art facility that would enhance revenues for the tenants, give fans a spectacular experience, and save money for the owner and tenants during both construction and operation.

Steve Patterson believes that the Siemens team accomplished its objectives:

"We had significant cost savings because of the great efficiencies of combining the different systems. The 'one-stop shopping' also helped in terms of timing, meeting tight schedule deadlines. We anticipate even greater savings in the operation of the stadium. Siemens understood how to integrate the various operating systems and provided a more holistic approach to managing the construction and the operational side. It would have been much more difficult if we had had to coordinate all of the subcontractors."

Scope of the Project

Reliant Stadium was designed to be an advanced entertainment center. The stadium is located in a campus-like setting of 350 acres. The stadium and its companion exhibition hall, the 1.4-million-square-foot Reliant Center, both use state-of-the-art telecommunications, fiberoptic networking switchgear, and intelligent control systems for comfort, fire safety, security, and lighting, each provided by Siemens as part of its integrated solution.

Communicating the Vision

Arkison knew that developing this highly competitive proposal would be a team effort: "Each member of our team did as much research as possible within our respective specialties to build a sound, cohesive, and smart proposal. We went beyond the customers' requirements in preparing for the presentation because we were trying to create a different approach to selling in this market. We knew we could no longer cut prices. We had to be creative in how we sold the project, maintaining a reasonable profit for Siemens while providing good value to the customer. The key was combining all of the divisions of our company. By doing this, we took ourselves out of the competitors' realm."

The team held fifteen- to thirty-minute face-to-face or phone meetings at least once a day to update everyone and identify and address potential problems. They asked three questions:

- What do we know?
- What has happened?
- What do we need to do next?

The team leader was the one point of contact with the customer.

Demonstrating They Were the Best Company for the Job

According to Arkison, "The most important thing we proved to them was that we had the team in place with the depth and breadth that was needed for a project of this scope. We presented to the whole construction team and proved that Siemens had an understanding of the project that went far beyond that of other companies. And we brought more advanced and sophisticated technology to the project.

"Our value proposition was that Siemens would provide the customers a single point of contact and develop a partnership, not just a contract. This evolved to the point where the customer considered our ability to manage a complex project within a tight time frame as the strongest value of our proposal."

Steve Patterson supports this contention. "They coordinated a complicated project on a fast track while the rest of the complex was also under construction—not an easy task."

An Important Lesson

When the Siemens team first started out, they were enthusiastic about their approach. But one of the challenges they faced early on was that the customers, and even Siemens's own internal people, had reservations about whether the integrated approach was a realistic idea.

Owen Arkison said, "We needed to create a new mind-set with the customer. We spent a year trying to convince them that we had a good approach, and then we realized we needed to adjust what we were saying slightly, to fit it into the norm they already accepted and practiced. Later, we approached the business the same way: instead of trying to change the whole process, we tailored it to fit within their existing mind-set."

Internal Barriers

While the Siemens team was ultimately successful, success wasn't guaranteed. Internal barriers were potentially a big issue because the sales team was creating a new approach. Like many organizations, Siemens had people who were comfortable doing things a certain, perhaps traditional, way, but Arkison said they were able to overcome this resistance. "First we started picking people who had the vision and the right attitude, then we broke the vision down into smaller components, so they saw they *could* do it. Otherwise, the big picture was too big. We had to keep it in their comfort zone. We had to adjust our approach internally just as we had externally."

The Foundation for Success

According to Arkison, there were two fundamental elements that inspired success: the team was highly motivated, and they had the right attitude about the project. Their attitude, he believes, was created by the exciting vision, their commitment to that vision, their creative thinking about how to achieve it, and the excitement of actually doing it. "These people have been in business a long time, and have done the same thing over and over. In this case, it was something different, something new." Arkison said he hated to use the term, but "thinking out of the box" and then making it happen was what enabled them to succeed.

Siemens had just begun offering this kind of integrated approach to its customers, and developing a full-scale plan of this size and complexity was different for the company. It was an ambitious departure from the existing way of doing business for them, for their customer, and even for their industry. Sales executives had discussed bringing their many different divisions under one contract at other times, but they found that people needed time to accept the idea. "It's a credit to management and to the people here that, as large a company as Siemens is, once we made the decision to go to market this way we were able to make this change and do it quickly," Arkison noted.

As a result of the innovative approach and success with this project, Siemens now looks to its sales professionals to be business development managers for integrated solutions. They have also created a new company, Siemens One, to coordinate such integrated designs.

Fundamentals of Business Case Development

If you uncover an opportunity for an innovative solution that your company doesn't currently offer, depending on the nature of the solution, you may need to work with your marketing, product management, and financial people to present a business case to get backing to move ahead. The larger, the more unique, and the riskier the sale, the more likely it is that you will need some type of business case.

If you are going to be involved in presenting a business case, it's important to thoroughly prepare the case. If the sale is a significant one, it will be worth the effort you'll invest. The more complete and compelling your case, the more likely it is that you will win approval and that you will also get the internal support you'll need to implement the solution.

The following are key items you'll want to include in your business case:

- A description of the business problem or opportunity
- An overview and details of the proposed solution(s), including
    - whether the solution is an extension of an existing product or service (less costly)
    - whether the solution will have application to other customers (less costly)

- the unique customer benefits of the proposed solution
  (and proposed pricing) and customer perceived value
- the strategic fit with current and future business plans and
  alternatives considered
- a financial analysis for the proposed solution(s)
- A competitive assessment (Are competitive options available?)
- Assumptions and issues (What scenarios have been considered?)
- Key success factors, such as risks of going ahead versus not going
  ahead, contrary views

According to Steve Celic, a product manager with experience at several large companies, "You have to have solid numbers, both quantitatively and qualitatively, to get buyoff from management, and your assumptions need to be well supported. It used to be that if the numbers weren't strong, you could still make your case strategically, but that's no longer true." He stresses that "upper-level managers are now 'all from Missouri' when it comes to financial expectations in business cases, and increasingly, CFOs track results because experience has shown that these projections tend to be optimistic. Given past results, approvals aren't easy to get. Companies want immediate cash flow and would rather invest in several bigger programs than a lot of smaller ones. Typically, companies like to get their money back in the first year, and few will look out more than three."

Product managers are typically going to view this in a similar way. With limited resources, they will want a solution that's right not just for the customer, but also for the company. If it's not right for the company, why do it?

While you may have a high hurdle to clear in presenting a convincing business case, once you do the momentum will be on your side.

In developing your proposal, build relationships with the right people in the customer's organization, the community of key decision makers and decision influencers who make the buying decision, define requirements, or control budgets. They may be in a number of different organizations, including operations, marketing, or even supply chain organizations.

If what you're seeking is going to have wider application with other customers, it may be possible to make it a standard part of your product offering. That will help lower costs and make it more attractive financially.

Celic also cautions salespeople to be careful about establishing understandings to provide something other than what's formally been agreed to. He noted that in trying to get the sale or accommodate the customer, salespeople might undermine their company's ability to meet the customer's expectations, or do it profitably. As a salesperson, you are representing your company and need to negotiate for your company's interests.

Creating a New Relationship

Bayer Polyurethane has developed a program that has led to long-term partnering relationships. This is not just a way for Bayer to sell its raw materials; more important, it's a way to give the customer extra value, according to Charles Valentine, national sales director.

Bayer Polyurethane accomplishes this through an agreement that increases its usage and their linkage to the customer. This arrangement provides the customer with additional support and access to Bayer's technology. It also helps improve the customer's product and manufacturing process. In this relationship, the technology door is open; Bayer shares technology with the customer that would be held close to the vest within a normal business relationship for fear that the technology could be used with a competitor's materials.

A team came up with this new approach. At first, it was met with customer reluctance. Some of the customer's people considered Bayer's effort intrusive. They were protective of their own technology and way of doing things. They said, "We will solve our own problems." Convincing the customer to be open to this new approach wasn't easy, but Bayer worked hard to convince the customers that it had a vast number of resources that could help them solve their problem.

Valentine offered the following advice based on how Bayer developed this new relationship:

- *Identify the value of what you are proposing.* Find the real value by presenting options and assessing how the customer reacts. Look at where the customer's focus is. For example, selling is tough in certain markets because of the move toward lean structures. Look for ways to make the customer's job easier by fitting in with that lean structure rather than fighting it.
- *Sell and create a relationship that increases your value.* Move toward a partnership model so that both parties begin to realize that the win-win scenario is real. We want to arrive at the point where the customer says, "I couldn't envision doing business without you." As you attempt to forge a new relationship, recognize that the customer may not be receptive at first. Plan how you will manage the change in the relationship.
- *Raise the level of professionalism of your salespeople.* Let them all know that they are salespeople *and* businesspeople. They need to manage the business with the customer. This includes understanding how the customer operates, what their market perspective is, whether they are leaders or price buyers, and what is their payment history.

Valentine says, "American businesses used to be innovators; but too often today, businesses try to save their way into prosperity. Instead of managing their business, they manage costs. I don't know what the solution is, but we have to keep remembering that there is a business behind every decision. The bottom line is the value of the long-term relationship. For us it means knowing where 90 percent of our capacity is going, which is significant for our business."

Communication

One of the other things that Valentine's salespeople do is to have what they call "commercial discussions" prior to technical discussions. They want to be able to prove to the customer the value of their proposal on a business basis before they prove it in on a technical basis.

Members of the Bayer sales force may communicate different things to different people, depending on their function, but they communicate the same core messages to each, such as the value of the innovative approach they are proposing. Valentine says, "One of the keys is if you're going to invest a half million dollars in a project and you are talking with marketing and they don't have a marketing plan, then you don't have a commitment. The customer's internal communications may not be all that good."

He continues, "This approach helps expands our customers' market and thereby increases our own; it should lead to a long-term arrangement. There are benefits to planning and partnering this way, and one of them is the intangible cost of switching vendors or customers. The costs of switching are not a line item, so you don't want the customer to overlook them."

The approach Bayer uses today is, "Let's see if we can find more innovative ways to increase our comfort level in revealing the technology." Valentine says the real issue is not a matter of mistrust; it's that people change positions and larger corporations are multidimensional, so not everyone may be aware of the value you bring. "There are different departments within the customer's organization, and each can pull in separate directions. If purchasing is measured on reduction in cost, how do they justify paying a higher price? And could they perceive you as taking away their job? Even upper management has to justify the difference. We use constant communications to all levels and across all departments to inform people about the value of what we bring and to keep people up to date."

According to Valentine, Bayer has always sold technology, but the difference was that most times a supplier and customer would reveal as little as possible about the technology. They would try to incorporate technology into the product in such a way that the customer couldn't misappropriate it for use with another supplier.

The Core of Law 4: Build Relationships for Repeat Business

A business relationship is not a personal relationship, and building that business relationship is a critical part of your job.

PART II

TAKE THE LEAD

FIND THE LIMITS AND THEN EXCEED THEM BY OWNING INNOVATIVE CUSTOMER SOLUTIONS

Law 5: Start with a Leader's Perspective
Law 6: Lead from Within
Law 7: Make It a Team Effort

"A leader inspires people to change rather than forcing them to change."
—Jim DeSena

START WITH A LEADER'S PERSPECTIVE

What can you do as a sales professional to be sure you will succeed consistently over time? There is a principle to start with that we will examine in this chapter.

The Sales Leadership Principle

Sales leaders rely on individual qualities of success to lead their organizations in developing innovative customer solutions. The model described here has three parts, each part of *sales leadership success* building on the earlier one. *Sales* is a matter of serving customers. *Leadership* is a matter of serving colleagues (employees or other team members). *Success* is a matter of being of service to our families, our communities, and ourselves. To stand out in sales, you need skills, knowledge, and talent. But you also must be able to influence the customer, your organization, and the people who support you. That requires leadership. To be a great leader, you need to build on a solid base of individual success. The top row in figure 5 shows each part of the performance process. The bottom row shows the people who benefit.

Sales leaders engage people to go in new directions at levels beyond what they thought possible, and do it with consistent performance. Sales leaders become exceptional by continually striving to learn and develop, to break through their own limits. Leaders encourage change. They are the catalysts for inspiring other people to rise above their limits,

Figure 5

Sales	Leadership	Success
Customers	Colleagues	Self

to rise to meet a challenge and do more than they thought possible. The first step to breaking through limits is to see a vision of what is possible, believe it can be achieved, and then believe in the people who must make it a reality. Sales leaders envision such breakthroughs for their customers. They get their organizations as excited as they are about the possibilities of delivering innovative solutions that address customer problems. They line up support to implement the solution and work to prevent or correct any implementation problems that occur. This is how sales leaders are able to deliver high-value, innovative customer solutions.

Sales Leadership Success Starts with Individual Qualities of Success

To be a great leader, you have to build on individual qualities of success. Let's test this principle. To be a person with individual qualities of success, you have to possess strength of character—integrity (doing what you say), identity (knowing your strengths), and values that allow you to model the behaviors of success you expect from others. You have to overcome potential or real weaknesses that can detour your success. For example, think of someone who has a strong product or technical background but who is not comfortable in managing relationships. That may be a limitation depending on how often the person must be involved with others. While everyone doesn't need to possess every possible quality, people often stand out because they excel in one or two character traits that others come to know and trust them for.

Strong leaders have a solid understanding of themselves. They have a firm grip on such areas as self-awareness, self-discipline, self-confidence, self-development, and self-control. To lead others to greatness, start with a foundation of personal success.

To Be an Outstanding Sales Professional, You Will Influence Others

A leader is someone who inspires others to action rather than forcing them into it. People who rely on position, threats, or manipulation may get what they want in the short term, but they will burn too many bridges to be around for the long term. Outstanding salespeople develop relationships with customers. The exceptional sales leader is often called upon to influence his or her organization to go beyond established routines and accepted practices, products, or services to meet customer needs. Exceptional sales leaders are able to get internal staff (marketing, IT, accounting, design, support, and so on) to provide outstanding service to their customers because they provide outstanding service to their internal staff. They treat them with respect, don't ask them to do anything they wouldn't do themselves, and recognize their expertise. When problems arise, the inside staff will go the extra mile for the sales leader who goes the extra mile for them and recognizes their efforts.

Look for the Win-Win-Win Solution

An outstanding salesperson helps customers take advantage of opportunities in a win-win-win approach (a win for the customer, a win for the salesperson, a win for the salesperson's company). Exceptional sales leaders do not accept the status quo without question, but look at things the way they are and question why they shouldn't or couldn't be better. To be able to sell effectively, you must be able to influence the customer and others. *Some salespeople are more interested in what they have to sell than what the customer wants to buy.* It's not easy putting your interests aside in favor of the customer's, especially when you're excited about what you offer or focused on how much money the sale is worth.

Begin at the Beginning

The limits to our success lie within us. Because they do, we can conquer those limits by understanding what they are and compensating for them. A leader builds on a base of individual strengths. A leader inspires others to action, getting them to make decisions or resolve problems when necessary. Exceptional sales leaders draw on sales skills and leadership abilities to deliver innovative solutions to customers and their organizations.

The Sales Leader's Challenge

The sales leader's challenge is

- To take the initiative
- To not accept the status quo when the present way of serving customers is less than it could be
- To inspire others to follow his or her vision for achieving what seems to be impossible
- To maintain confidence and control in the face of crisis and uncertainty
- To provide communication, compassion, and direction when needed

"You can never accept the status quo."
—Jeffrey R. Immelt, chairman and CEO, General Electric

Sales leaders look at the status quo and question why things are the way they are. They search for ways to tackle what others might consider tolerable or acceptable. They find innovative solutions.

Change Requires Leadership

In times of change, people need to do things differently to accommodate or take advantage of those changes. When necessary, leaders initiate change to create better solutions. They may effect change within their organizations even if it doesn't seem apparent to everyone that those changes are necessary: if they think it makes sense to change the business model or the way they are organized to serve customers, they will. If they have an exciting vision for serving customers in innovative ways, they will champion those changes for the customers. Getting people aligned around those changes is a leadership role.

Figure 6

Change ▮▮➡ Leadership

Leaders not only take advantage of change, they encourage it. They look for the opportunities it creates and encourage others to do likewise.

If we were to think about the rate of change—how much more quickly things change today as opposed to yesterday—and plot change over time on a graph, it might look something like figure 7. Change is accelerating, and it will continue to do so. It is driven by science and technology and by information that is ever more widely and quickly available. It is driven by human curiosity and inventiveness.

When individuals or organizations are young, they tend to accept new technology easily. For example, children quickly adapt to video games and computers. But once individuals or organizations become comfortable with that technology and get older, they often don't read-

Figure 7

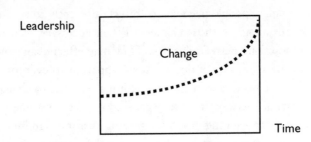

ily accept new technology. Knowing this tendency and being able to not get caught in that limited way of thinking is a competitive advantage.

The Process of Change

There is a predictable pattern to the process of change, as shown below. The key is to not get endlessly stuck fighting what you or others see as an undesirable change but to instead work through it to see how you can turn it to your advantage.

- Denial: Why is this happening (to me)?
- Resistance: Whom can I blame?
- Acceptance: How can I make the best of this?
- Transition: What can I do to adapt?
- Performance: Where can I make a difference?
- Growth: When do I need to change again?

Use the following questions to think about your customers and their businesses.

- How have your customers changed?
- In what ways are your customers' needs changing?
- How have their customers changed?

For example, how have things such as technology, information processing, communications, cultural diversity, pricing, cost, pressures, security, workforce education, competition, globalization, the economy, and the Internet affected your customers? Think of how they have affected you or your company.

To what extent does the customer perceive these changes? How well has this person's company taken advantage of those changes? What does he or she think will happen in the next year? What impact might it have on the company? In what ways has the customer responded to these changes? In what other ways can he or she respond? Is something preventing a response?

> *"We try to anticipate the next change, because change is the medium of opportunity."*
> —James C. Morgan, chairman and CEO, Applied Materials

If You're Not Part of the Solution, You're Part of the Problem

Sales leaders are part of the solution because they strive to understand the customer's business. Sales leaders become experts in their industry, their company, and their products or services. They are experts at solving problems and identifying opportunities, continually developing and using these skills. They choose to develop their expertise in depth so that customers can count on them to offer innovative solutions.

Initiate, Influence, Inspire

Sales leaders make their presence known by initiating, influencing, and inspiring. Initiating discussions with customers, they get things started rather than waiting to be told what to do. They influence not only people in the customer's organization but people in their own organization. They influence others by how they communicate their ideas for the customer. They work to create understanding, enthusiasm, and support in their organization. They respect others' concerns and respond to them. They inspire others when the going gets rough by reminding people about the original objectives and the results they will bring to the customers, and by being in the trenches when needed.

In a highly competitive environment, you want to always be the person your customers think about first when they think about calling in someone to help them. Keeping "front of mind" involves initiating, influencing, and inspiring:

- *Initiate.* Challenge the status quo—look for opportunities to grow your business by helping your customers grow theirs. Understand the customer's business challenges and strategies. Be alert to changes in sales (slight falloffs that could be precursors to bigger losses). Monitor customer costs. (If you don't proactively look for ways to reduce them, someone else will.)
- *Influence.* Demonstrate how you are committed to your customers and influence them to be as committed to you. Demonstrate how you provide them with unique products, service, support, or pricing. (Do you sell to everyone, or are you selective? What would your customers lose if they were no longer your customers? What do your customers see as the benefits of working with you?)
- *Inspire.* Leaders inspire people to do things. Tell a story about how your company stood by a customer in tough times; how you went the extra mile when a customer needed service; how you went way beyond a customer's expectations. Give people a solid reason to be emotionally comfortable with and committed to relying on you.

Every Change Presents an Opportunity

You have to find opportunity in change. And if the change appears at first to be negatively affecting you, finding that opportunity will present a bigger challenge. The reason is your frame of mind. If you perceive the change as a threat, you are going to be looking for ways to defend yourself against that threat rather than finding ways to take advantage of it. Or you may downgrade the threat, thinking it will affect others but not you. History is replete with examples of this, but the most recent example is the Internet.

When the Internet first appeared, more established companies weren't certain what it was or how to take advantage of it. Some of them dismissed it as a nonevent. New companies that were started because of the Internet found ways to take advantage of it, such as using it as a distribution channel for merchandise (Amazon, eBay), not just for information. Once the more established companies saw the advantages of the Internet for selling, cost reduction, or customer contact, they brought enormous resources to the table. While many of the original dot-com companies were founded on good concepts, they weren't run well as businesses and ran out of funds when reality set in. Those with good business models that took advantage of the Internet and had good leadership survived.

If you put time and energy into defending against something, it's not at all likely that you will see how to turn the threat to your advantage. If you dismiss it and it turns out to be a viable threat to your business, you will then have to play catchup. A better course of action is to have a separate group develop a plan to build a business opportunity around change.

Clayton Christensen, in his book *The Innovator's Dilemma*, describes a principle of successful technology transition: it's difficult for successful companies to exploit major changes in technology (and keep growing). Companies that have been successful with one technology find it difficult to take advantage of what Christensen calls *disruptive technology*, technology that takes a leap forward, because at first their customers don't need it and the companies don't see the same profit potential in it as they have with their existing products. New companies, not bound by the existing paradigms, capitalize on the disruptive technology. They go after the customers the existing company won't pursue, but after these other companies improve the technology and it becomes more cost effective to mainstream customers, they are able to move up to capture customers who initially rejected the technology. (These are customers of the larger, more successful companies, whose existence is threatened by the new technology and the companies that are exploiting it.)

Salespeople and their organizations run into the same issues when confronted with something new. How they respond determines their future.

> *"It may look like we are going around in circles, but we are climbing a spiral staircase."*
> —Niklas Savander, vice president, Nokia

Three Roles of Sales Leaders

There are three roles of a sales leader in creating a climate for change:

- Challenge the status quo.
- Create and communicate an exciting vision.
- Support, encourage, and recognize those pursuing that vision.

Getting what you need for your customers may mean initiating change at your own company. That will mean that you will have to make a case for why your proposal is essential to keeping your customer's business, and perhaps the business of other customers.

You may need to demonstrate how your customer's business is unique, how it has changed, or how the current solution doesn't fit the present needs of the customer or is more costly or slower than what your competition offers. Your business case will need to describe projected revenues under several scenarios. You may want to seek input from your design or engineering people as you get further along to demonstrate feasibility and costs and to garner their support for your proposal. You will probably have to sell your proposal more convincingly up your own line and across to other departments than you will to your customer. Your customer will probably quickly see the advantages of what you offer. You may find that your company is protecting its vested interests. Some companies are receptive to new ideas, but others prefer the status quo. In the latter, you will need to do more to help your idea prevail. You can make a good case if you offer convincing data and win the support of one person at a time. Find an influential person you think would be receptive to your idea. Once you win him or her over, you will find less resistance when you go to the next person and say that so-and-so is on board.

Some battles you will win, and some you won't. The key is to make sure you do a thorough analysis and then build support. Knowing when to forge ahead is a matter of experience, balancing the likelihood of selling your idea in your organization and the potential payoff with the time you'll need to invest.

Challenge the Status Quo

Sales leaders look for opportunities to do things differently when they see a potential benefit for the customer. They can play within the rules to accomplish what they see as necessary. One of the salespeople I know came in to take over an existing customer account. The customer had $50,000 worth of unused products that he wanted to return. The vendor didn't normally make refunds, but the salesperson looked at the situation creatively and came up with a solution that was agreeable to both the customer and the company. Rather than just going back to the customer and telling the customer what couldn't be done, he looked for a way to keep the customer's future business and maintain support within the company. This wasn't a big challenge to the status quo, but these types of initiatives can spell the difference between keeping and losing the customer. Lose a customer here and a customer there and it adds up. Even one is one too many if there is a way to reasonably accommodate the customer's concerns.

Create and Communicate an Exciting Vision

Quality is delivering what was promised to the customer. Most companies strive to deliver a quality product or service. Not all succeed. While it is not the salesperson's job to deliver the product, sales leaders leave nothing to chance. They may not oversee every step of the delivery process, but they are not going to be surprised by a call from an upset customer complaining about a late or wrong shipment. They want assurance that the product or service is delivered on time and as promised. They stake their credibility on it. They will get to the right people if there is a problem and convince them that it is in everyone's best interest for them to quickly rectify the problem. They won't fix it themselves except in rare cases, but they will make sure it is fixed. Especially for new accounts or new orders, they will keep oversight of the customer's order throughout the process, or have someone they trust do it, and head off a problem before it occurs. Again, while this is not written into their job, they know that customer goodwill, referrals, and future sales are going to depend on everything going without a hitch.

It's not enough just to have a great vision. That idea has to be communicated to people in a way that they can understand and internalize so they can act on it. It is a matter of building a base of support for implementing the vision. Communication needs to take place in a variety of ways and forums to reinforce the message. Once may not be enough.

Support, Encourage, and Recognize Those Pursuing That Vision

Regardless of whether you are working on a short-term sale or a long-term, bigger sale, you need to ensure that people who work on the proposal are able to contribute according to their unique talents. This means that you must create the kind of environment where people are willing to go beyond the day-to-day ways of doing things so that your team can make a difference for the customer.

How do you create a growth environment? Here are three ways.

- Do what you can to ensure that you take advantage of the skills and motivation that people bring to the table. What skills or attitudes do you need on your sales team for it to be successful? What unique skills can each team member contribute? Ask.
- Make sure that people communicate effectively, whether that is through face-to-face meetings or through video or audio conferences, with E-mail, instant messaging, briefings, or memos.

- When you win a new account, make a big or unusual sale, or lose a sale, debrief the event. What helped? What didn't? Capture the relevant points so that people won't make the same mistake again.

NNR Aircargo Service (USA) Inc. is an international air cargo shipper. NNR won an account with a large medical equipment manufacturer with worldwide distribution and has provided service to that manufacturer for a number of years. The customer told NNR he liked their service because they are "proactive, finding ways to remove the roadblocks to inefficiencies that other shippers may accept as the way of doing business." I asked Andy Hadley, global accounts manager, how his company knows enough not to accept the status quo. He said: "We sit down and listen to customer requirements. At first, most of the time, you hear, 'Everything is fine.' But then we ask, 'Is there something that your current supplier isn't doing that you expect?' In this case, the customer said, 'Our present supplier won't deviate out of their norm; there is no flexibility.' We saw that as an opportunity, and we told them we could do it the way they wanted. This particular company sets the bar high for us, in terms of what they expect, but we like that because we're able to jump over it. We've got a good process in place now, but we always have to be willing to step back and change it. We have to remain flexible."

Flexibility in meeting customer needs was the key to success in this case. It is a competitive advantage that NNR Aircargo relies on. That flexibility relies on an attitude of being open to doing things differently than the "normal" way. Too many suppliers get caught up in doing things their way and aren't open to customizing their service to the customer. Larger companies especially can find it difficult to do things differently from the norm because they often focus on standardizing service and being efficient. That stance gives more flexible companies an opening into the account.

Salespeople can fall into the same trap when they have a predetermined agenda for what they want to sell the customer. When the customer responds with a different need, they argue for their solution instead of trying to understand what the customer really wants. It's an easy trap to fall into. But if you're going to be successful, you have to be able to put aside your attachment to a certain solution and find another one that still works for the customer. Listening and empathy are key to being able to do that.

Sales Leaders See the Reality

Leaders are always watching for changes and opportunities that their customers can take advantage of. They do this by interacting with customers; listening to feedback from the people closest to the customers, the sales and service people; working with the engineers and research people; and looking at trends in business. The leaders may not always be the first ones to identify the opportunity, but if they aren't they will encourage others to do so and then listen to their ideas.

Know What Customers Need Before They Do

Sales leaders know from years of experience and understanding what works and what doesn't. They know never to wait to be told something that they should already know. Companies don't thrive by simply meeting their customers' needs in the current marketplace. That quickly becomes a competitive disadvantage. Getting out ahead of the market— knowing what customers need before they do—is a strategy that leaders use. That strategy drives decisions that affect everything the customer does, including growth, personnel, and products. Understanding what customers need before they do requires having a strong presence and understanding of their business while being able to step back and look objectively at their situation. Your objectivity, coupled with your expertise, will allow you to see things that people who are close to the problem and who don't possess your expertise won't see.

> *"We're not interested in just planting our flag in every country to say we're global. If you stay at that first level of functionality—you make washers, people have dirty clothes everywhere—you can go anywhere in the world. But the second questions is 'How can we go in and make money?'"*
>
> —Lloyd Ward, chairman and CEO of Maytag Corporation

What Followers Want from Leaders

What are the two most important qualities that followers want from leaders? James M. Kouzes and Barry Z. Posner conducted a study and published their findings in their book *The Leadership Challenge*. The two qualities that followers most wanted from leaders were *honesty* and *competency*. Note that both of these qualities relate to trust. In effect, people want to be led by someone they can trust, someone they know will do the best thing and not lead them down a path that goes nowhere. Customers want the same thing. They want to trust their salesperson to handle their relationship with honesty and competency. They want a leader.

Prove Them Wrong

The next time you are faced with a situation where people aren't convinced you can accomplish something, rather than arguing, sulking, or retreating, prove them wrong. Tap into the enormous reserve of knowledge and strength that lies within you, develop a plan, and then move ahead smartly with a focused determination to accomplish your goal, always maintaining a positive attitude.

> *"Probably the biggest thing Lou Gerstner did for our company was get us focused on our customers. He started by building a mind-set that says everything we do helps our customers compete more effectively and win in their marketplace. That's the foundation."*
>
> —Ned Lautenbach, senior vice president
> of sales and distribution, IBM

Account Managing Versus Account Leading

Let's look at the difference between managing and leading. The two terms are sometimes used interchangeably—such as when people refer to someone in a management position as a leader—but there are important distinctions.

The difference between managing and leading is the difference between doing things right versus doing the right things. Doing things right means being efficient. Doing the right things means being effective. Sales leaders are *efficient* when they get quotes and other work done quickly. They are *effective* when they are calling on the right companies and the right people.

Sales leaders really need a combination of both attributes. You need to do *the right things right*. You need a combination of effectiveness and efficiency. In either case, if you are ineffective or inefficient, you can be out of business.

Account managers tend to an account. Account leaders create business. They line up support behind their proposals. They create support and commitment. They create excitement.

Leadership requires aligning and enabling people. The objective is to create options for effectively handling unpredictable situations. Leadership is focused on developing capabilities to address multiple scenarios and to have the right individuals embrace the challenges of identifying and executing those scenarios.

The differences in results between managing and leading are like the differences between night and day. And, just like night and day, we need both. We need leadership in times of change. The more change there is, the more leadership we need. The more change that has to take place, the more we need leaders. Yet we also need to be able to manage our resources wisely.

The key for any leader is to be adaptable enough to recognize when he or she needs to use a different style and to work comfortably in that style. The people who have the most difficulty are the ones who get locked into a style that is not the best one for the situation they face or the people they are working with. The people who are the most successful are those with the self-confidence and skills to adapt to new market requirements and who can inspire others to follow them.

Leadership or Loyalty?

Some people confuse leadership and loyalty, thinking that if you follow their directions you have leadership ability. It doesn't take a lot of thinking, decision making, or initiative to follow directions—it takes *loyalty*. Managers usually value loyalty, even above competency. It's not surprising when you think about it. If you gave someone instructions to do something and he or she didn't do it quite right, you would give the person credit for at least following your directions. But if you instructed someone to do something and that person not only intentionally didn't do what you asked but also didn't tell you about not doing it, your reaction would be different. You would be mystified, annoyed, or worse. But that reaction is provoked by an offense to your sense that the person should be loyal to you, not by your estimation of the person's leadership skills.

In a military operation, people need to follow directions or there will be confusion and loss. But even in the military, a commander must be able not only to follow orders but to communicate, initiate, and inspire the troops to do their best when it's most difficult to do so.

Sometimes, people choose not to follow a particular directive but still get the results the director wanted. In that case, their indiscretion will likely be overlooked. In fact, it may be seen as "being resourceful." This trait may be valued because the person is still supporting the company in accomplishing an objective, even though he or she may not have done it in a conventional way. You could say the person was demonstrating an aspect of leadership. People will say about these situations "It is easier to beg forgiveness than it is to ask permission." That's true as long as you get the results.

Some bosses don't even go this far in granting people the autonomy to figure out how to do their jobs. They micromanage. They take away the person's ability to lead, to make independent decisions. The boss suffers and so does the organization, because micromanaging results in suboptimal solutions. As a sales leader, you need to encourage your support team to use their creative talents to get the job done and to let you know if they have a better way of doing it. You may still want them to do it, if it is within your authority, and as the salesperson that is your prerogative. You will expect them to carry out the decision knowing that they had a chance to influence the decision.

Find a Greater Good

To inspire and create the will to succeed and persevere, in yourself and others, find a greater good. Look for something that goes beyond the immediate or the ordinary, something that will matter, that will leave a legacy. Focus your attention on benefiting others. The motivation to succeed can be multiplied many times by the belief in something bigger than any individual.

Jean is a successful sales engineer with an eighteen-year track record with a leading medical device company. She sells to physicians. When she was first appointed to her position, she realized a change was needed.

She said, "We needed to educate our customers, the doctors, about the benefits of our technology. We had great relationships with them, but they weren't able to take advantage of all we had to offer because they didn't realize our products could do things that other treatments, such as medication, couldn't." Jean saw that being great friends with the doctors wasn't enough. This observation, along with her decision to do things differently, epitomizes sales leadership. A problem became an opportunity for her and her company to create a win-win-win scenario: doctors could better serve their patients; Jean's company could expand their business; and Jean could do more of what she had been put in the job to do—solve problems for her customers. The effect of this was that the doctors could use more advanced methods to help their patients enjoy and extend their lives. She could sell more, serve her customers, and support the goals of her company, all within the context of a greater good. Look for the greater good in what you do. It will give you the ability to influence others to get done what needs to be done without having to direct them to do it.

Leaders create change to better serve their customers. They create change internally to get people to do what needs to be done to bring innovative solutions to customers. They communicate, influence, and convince people to adjust to and accommodate changing customer requirements. They are pragmatists. They don't try to change things for change's sake. They have an end result in mind: delivering solid solutions to customers.

Sales leaders are not simply the top producers. They are professionals who change how they work to fit the changing needs of their customers and who bring about the changes needed internally to meet or exceed those customer requirements. Sales leaders are able to consistently deliver over a period of many years by continually adapting to changing customer requirements. They may or may not always be the top producers, but usually they are.

While marketing and sales may have customers as their reason for being, they can find themselves working at cross purposes. When that begins to happen, sales leaders recognize it and use their ability to influence internally just as they would to influence customers. They recognize that they and marketing must work together closely if their company is to be successful. They strive to overcome their differences by finding their common interests. They work to achieve a delicate balance between the needs of their customers and the needs of the company. They navigate through these requirements with firmness and tact.

Instituting change inside any organization can be an enormous challenge, one that can take much longer than expected or be ultimately unsuccessful. How can you, as a sales professional, get people inside your company to be open to a new idea or a different approach? One excellent way is to enlist them in the effort. This is similar to what you do in asking customers questions to uncover their business needs—you enlist them in identifying the problem and possible solutions. They are then more willing to make a decision because they were instrumental in coming up with the solution. You, as an expert, guided them toward it.

Business 2.0's January 2002 issue provided an account of the turnaround that took place at Nissan Motors. In the fiscal year ending in March 2001, Nissan posted their first annual profit in four years and the biggest ever in their sixty-eight-year history. Three years earlier, Renault had bought a stake in the faltering company and brought in Carlos Ghosn to turn things around.

Nissan had their traditional ways of working. Ghosn needed to win the commitment of Nissan's people to dramatic changes. He got them involved by setting up nine cross-functional teams. (Members were selected on the basis of their commitment to change.) These teams ultimately produced two thousand proposals that cut debt and costs. Nissan also introduced new car designs that sold well.

The changes saved the company, and did it quickly. Ghosn said, "One of the greatest successes in business is to do what people say you cannot do."

Sales leaders, both within their company and even within a customer's organization, must fight lethargy, complacency, and inertia to bring about change.

Sales Leaders Create Momentum

Why is it that people don't switch to another company when they are dissatisfied with their present vendor? Why is it that people continue doing the same thing long after it has outlived its usefulness? The short answer is *inertia*. People will stay with a vendor because they see it as being too inconvenient, too costly, or too time consuming to switch, as long as the problem with the vendor doesn't exceed a certain threshold: that is, the point at which the pain of staying with the vendor is greater than the pain of switching. People will continue doing the same thing, going along the same path, until it becomes more painful to continue doing what they've been doing than to change.

Inertia is a term borrowed from physics—it means that a body at rest tends to stay at rest and a body in motion tends to stay in motion in a straight line unless acted upon by an outside force. People will endure minor or even major problems with a vendor they have been with for some time. The vendor will have built up a reserve of goodwill, so when there is a problem the customer perceives it as an anomaly and expects that it won't happen again. Of course, if a problem recurs, the reserve of goodwill can quickly evaporate. If the vendor corrects the problem the customer may stay with the vendor, but the damage may not be easily repaired.

Inertia works in favor of the present vendor. If you are the present vendor, you have a chance to correct the problem and keep the customer. If you are a new vendor trying to get an entry to a new customer, inertia works against you. But time may be on your side. If you keep in touch with the prospective customer, you may just get the chance to start providing some products or services as the customer tests your capabilities. If the old vendor really has major problems, you may be asked to take over completely and immediately. In either case, the way to make your opportunity is to be persistent, present, and in front of the customer's mind. Out of sight, out of mind, out of business.

Make inertia work for you. Make sure you don't give your customers a reason to be unhappy. Always be looking for ways to improve their level of satisfaction. Don't settle for the status quo. Be a leader and find ways to break through the limits of service that constrain other companies. If your customers love the service you provide, it would take a major change in personnel to unseat you as a preferred vendor.

If you are trying to land a new account, become the outside force that overcomes inertia. Look for ways that you can do things for the customer that the present vendor can't or won't do. At the very least, speak with the customer to find out about the current situation. Let the customer know that you would like an opportunity to be tested so that you could be available if he or she needs a second vendor. Be alert to changes in the customer's situation. Stay in touch so that one day when you make the call the customer will say, "I'm glad you called."

Create momentum for an idea or a change. People want to be associated with an exciting endeavor. They will become a part of something that is moving ahead, so you want to create momentum around a concept or plan you envisioned. That is the best way to get people to support you.

Change Happens Only When People Are Dissatisfied

Why would someone who is comfortable with the status quo be inclined to change? It doesn't happen. Lawrence Bossidy, former CEO of Honeywell, used the metaphor of a burning oil platform to illustrate what has to happen to rouse people from a state of comfort. People won't jump from an oil platform, which is high above the sea, if everything is OK. They see the risk of jumping from the platform as unacceptable. But what if they see smoke or feel heat from a fire? Bossidy's contention is that it is the job of a leader to shake people from complacency.

Bossidy offered IBM as an illustration of this principle. IBM had gone through a time when its sales were stagnating and it still considered itself to be primarily a mainframe computer manufacturer. Mainframe sales were soft because of the increase in the use of alternatives such as distributed processing through PCs. If IBM's people felt comfortable designing and selling mainframes, what incentive would they have to break out of their historical area of strength? They didn't realize that the "platform" (in this case, mainframes) was burning.

When Lou Gerstner came in as the new CEO, he talked to customers and employees and began a change in direction that has radically altered IBM's business profile while also building on its strengths.

IBM has always been known for exceptional service. The company was known for bringing in teams of people to the customer's location when needed to quickly fix problems. That level of assurance was one of the primary reasons people bought from IBM. While IBM might not have been best known for having leading-edge equipment, they were known for having leading-edge service.

IBM has evolved into a company that derives a major part of its revenues from services rather than products. It has also made consulting a significant part of its business. IBM provides the services a company needs as a package, which again provides that level of assurance for customers to know that they can continue their businesses virtually without interruption.

The problem in some organizations is that people are comfortable with the way things are. People who have experienced a great deal of change don't mind a period of stability. If that stability lasts beyond the time when things need to start changing, that company will begin to see its competitive advantage erode.

Value Innovation

Innovation is creativity channeled into productive use. Sales leaders look for opportunities to take a creative approach to problem solving and even finding problems. A study at Bell Laboratories on creativity sought to understand what led some people to be more creative than others.

What the study found as a common denominator was that creative people all *thought* they were creative. They approached problems in a creative manner and, as a result, were more likely to come up with creative solutions. They knew there could be multiple solutions to problems, so they looked for them. People who are creative are willing to tolerate, even encourage, the initial disorganization or confusion that creativity generates before it leads to concrete ideas.

Creative people use a variety of techniques to find creative solutions. The common factor, in many cases, is the ability to get engaged in an unrelated relaxing activity, letting the subconscious go to work to come up with solutions that the conscious mind could never imagine. Creative people tend to have an intense focus on their work, to get immersed in it, but they tackle diversions with just as much attention. Creative people also like to talk with other creative people and throw around ideas that lead to unexpected results.

I won't go so far as to claim that I'm a creative person, but I have my moments, and they tend to be when I'm relaxed and not actually thinking about a problem. It could be when I'm exercising, when I'm just awakening in the morning, or when I'm doing a completely unrelated activity. When you are facing what seems like an insurmountable problem and you have been working on it for some time, the best action might be to step away from it. That may seem counterintuitive, but it allows the subconscious to go to work.

MIT professor Eric Von Hippel suggests that companies work closely and continuously with their *lead users* in order to keep up with the changing needs of customers. Lead users are those who push the boundaries for solutions. Customers are often inventive with solutions, adapting what they use to better fit what they need. They may see needs that the supplier didn't when developing the product or service. Sales leaders can gain good insights by making their lead customers a priority when it comes to research and onsite presence.

But be careful when asking customers what they want. For example, when customers are asked what they would like, they say what they think they would like—but when they get it, it isn't what they want. What happened? The salesperson didn't probe and go beyond the initial request to find out what the real problems, desires, or needs were.

He might have looked at the symptom, but not the cause. He never identified the outcomes the individual wanted. He focused on processes and features, not benefits. He didn't observe how the customer actually used the product.

Creative people tend to draw on the right side of the brain for creative ideas and then use the left side of the brain to organize and implement. The right side works best when it is not working. You have probably gotten creative ideas and solutions when you weren't really thinking about them but instead were relaxed.

To develop innovative customer solutions means getting as much information as possible to frame the problem and then thinking creatively about what can be done to solve it. Creativity is like working out. You need to stretch your creative mind and build your creativity for it to be developed. Here are five suggestions for approaching problem solving creatively.

- *Be curious.* If something puzzles you or strikes you as unexpected, don't ignore it. Investigate it. What can you learn? What is unexplained? Why? Don't accept a quick, standard response to your query.
- *Challenge your beliefs.* What do you believe to be true? How might the situation or problem or solution be different from what you believe? What do others believe about the situation? Why? Suppose the opposite were true? Just because a belief is common doesn't make it true.
- *Follow your instincts.* If you feel something isn't right, it probably isn't. Look into it. Don't blindly follow the well-worn path without at least thinking about whether you want to. Be aware of boundaries and rules, but don't take them as the truth. Rules are for convenience; boundaries help control. Neither of those is helpful to creativity.
- *Consider all possibilities.* Don't reject a creative solution (or let someone else do it) by saying, "That will never work." If you prematurely reject an idea because it seems unfeasible, you may be rejecting the best solution before you've even evaluated it. At an early stage, don't focus on "how." If a solution is compelling, people will figure out how to make it work.

- *Ask the right questions.* When you encounter a roadblock, start asking, "Suppose . . . ?" Suppose we did this? Suppose we did that? You will encourage others to start thinking creatively along with you.

> *"Creativity in an organization starts where the action is—in the laboratory, in R and D sites, at a customer's place, in manufacturing."*
> —Samuel J. Palmisano, chairman and CEO, IBM

I call the use of creativity in a sales environment salesivity™. Salesivity gives you a powerful strategic advantage. It allows you to create solutions that uniquely position you with the customer and differentiate yourself from the competition.

Go Beyond the Boundaries

Creative solutions lie beyond the boundaries. Standard approaches are, by definition, within the boundaries, so if you are faced with a unique customer problem and need to come up with a unique customer solution, you will need to go beyond the boundaries. There is an inherent risk in doing so; success is not guaranteed and there could be a monetary cost or a perceived loss of power. But there is also an inherent risk in not doing so. The risk in not addressing the customer's unique problem in an innovative way is that someone else will.

Boundaries exist to limit options. In most cases, there is a relevant reason for this. If businesses didn't have budgets, for example, people would spend too little or too much. You need to respect ethical and legal boundaries (and take care not to push them). But when it's time to come up with *creative* solutions to customer problems, ways to do things better, faster, or cheaper, boundaries are the wrong place to start. The right place to start is by looking at what's *possible* or *desirable*, not what's feasible or manageable.

As many times as I have asked people to do the "nine-dot exercise," most people who haven't seen it before aren't able to come up with a solution (there is more than one), and about half the people who've seen a solution can't recall what it is. (The goal of the nine-dot exercise is to connect all nine dots in a pattern of three rows of three dots with only four straight lines without lifting your pen or pencil from the paper once you begin.) That's understandable. The key isn't really remembering the solution; it's remembering the principle behind the solution, which is what is often referred to as "thinking outside the box."

I hesitate to use this term, because it has become almost counterproductive to do so, but this is where classic *brainstorming* rules apply. There are two parts to the creative approach: The first is to generate as many ideas as possible within your given time frame. (The key here is to think quantity, not quality.) The second is to prioritize the solutions identified in the first step. (Now you think quality.) The difficulty often is that it isn't easy to stick with the rules, and unless you are actually in a formal creative session, people will often knock down a creative idea as soon as it is proposed.

It is up to you, the sales leader, to have a creative mind-set and explain to people ahead of time what you are striving to do so that you can create the right expectations on their part and then have a more effective creative dialogue. So even if you are having what may amount to an informal discussion of a problem and possible solutions, take care not to eliminate potential solutions before they have been given a chance to prove themselves.

Value Innovation and Growth

After analyzing more than thirty companies around the world, W. Chan Kim and Renee A. Mauborgne, in their paper "Value Innovation: The Strategic Logic of High Growth," found that the difference between the high-growth companies and their less successful competitors was in each group's assumptions about strategy. The less successful companies took a conventional approach: they sought to stay ahead of the competition. High-growth companies employed a strategy of offering unprecedented value. In essence, slower-growth companies compete with other companies. Higher-growth companies compete by challenging the status quo. The authors of the study suggest, "Most companies focus on matching and beating their rivals, and as a result their strategies tend to converge along the same basic dimensions of competition. As rivals try to outdo one another, they end up competing solely

on the basis of incremental improvements in cost or quality or both."
Value innovators question what an industry takes for granted.

A committee from The Industrial Research Institute, Inc., summarized the concept this way: "Value innovation is customer driven and the goal is a product or service with radically superior value. The innovation may use new or existing technology, but the solution usually does not follow conventional practices.

"Value innovations redefine the problems to:

- Discover hidden demand: expand the existing market
- Create new demand: identify new markets"

Put another way, technology innovation may or may not lead to greater value. It depends on what customers want.

Sales Leaders Create Value Innovation

Sales leaders apply these concepts in a sales environment by questioning the norms, standards, and assumptions that their customers, industries, or companies take for granted. Sales leaders gather information about the customer's situation, then step back and creatively assess what the situation is in the context of the customer's business goals and strategies. When they do this successfully, they will be in a position to deliver unique solutions to their customers. They will enlist the backing of a team of designers, engineers, or others in their efforts to develop the solution. Sales leaders aren't bystanders.

The High-Value Innovative Solutions Grid

A good way to understand the dimensions and differences of high- and low-value and innovative versus existing solutions is to place them in a grid I developed to help explain the concept. But let me begin by giving the definitions of *high-value* and *innovative solutions*.

High-value solutions are solutions that solve problems customers see as *high priority*, delivered *how* they want them. Innovative solutions are solutions that address or anticipate *changing* customer needs.

	Innovative solutions	Existing solutions
High value	1 Sales leaders	2 Sales professionals
Low value	3 Technologists	4 New salespeople

Thus, sales leaders, the consistent top producers, deliver high-value, innovative solutions, the combination shown in quadrant 1. Sales professionals deliver solutions built around high-value, existing products and services, shown in quadrant 2. Taking advantage of both existing and innovative solutions allows top producers to draw on the appropriate solution to meet a variety of customer needs and internal opportunities. Because innovative solutions require a larger investment of time and aren't always needed by the customer, using existing solutions for appropriate problems can be cost effective. But when existing solutions don't address the customer's changing needs or take advantage of new technologies to develop those needs, that's when sales leaders seek different or new applications.

Technologists provide innovative solutions to problems that customers see as low priority or deliver them in ways that are ineffective, as shown in quadrant 3. This is a solution looking for a problem.

Salespeople who work from existing solutions and just don't get to the right customer issues, if they make the sale at all, are going to provide low value from the customer's point of view. These salespeople, who are often new to the profession, are going to struggle to make higher-margin sales and develop repeat business (unless they start to deliver higher-value solutions). They are often going to have to compete on price and will spend a great deal of time trying to get a sale that ultimately won't lead to another sale. It will be difficult for them to remain in the business.

It is possible to go from quadrant 4 to 2—that is, to go from being a salesperson to being a sales professional. Salespeople who avail themselves of training, develop industry and business knowledge, and use a consultative approach to uncover customer needs can become sales professionals. It is possible to go from quadrant 3 to quadrant 1—from a technologist to a sales leader—but I suspect that the route is more likely to go from 3 to 2 and then to 1. This may be more likely if the individual understands what is missing and receives the support of his or her company to fill in the gaps. This is often the case in my sales workshops, when I have, for example, former engineers, designers, or IT people who sell. They have a strong technical background, and with the addition of the right selling skills they can become the sales professional, looking for customer problems first, not "data dumping" technical solutions on low-priority customer problems.

What are the distinctions between high and low value and between innovative and existing solutions?

High Value
- Solves high-priority customer problems
- Convenient and cost effective
- Consistent and assured results

Low Value
- Solves low-priority customer problems
- May be harder to use, requires extra time
- May not perform quite as promised

Innovative Solutions
- Address changing industry and market conditions
- Initiate a new perspective on old problems
- Use a new framework or new approaches

Existing Solutions
- Address current situation
- Use traditional approaches
- Use current framework

Innovation doesn't apply to technology alone. It can apply to the people side of the customer interaction. For example, you may want to look at the skills of people who work with your customer. Are their skills up to the level they need to be? Or does a lack of skills create errors or inconvenience for customers? Innovation can also apply to the customer process, which may or may not involve technology. If the customer, or people in the customer's organization, would find it beneficial to have a different arrangement for interfacing with your organization, accommodating that preference can lead to higher customer satisfaction.

Remember that innovative salespeople do the following consistently:

- Ask "What if?"
- Use creative thinking time
- Don't first ask "How?" but "Why?"
- Have a balance between results and process
- Give credit to others when deserved

The Core of Law 5: Start with a Leader's Perspective

The more change there is, the more leadership is needed, and a sales leader helps his or her customers take advantage of change by creating a vision for a customer solution and then inspiring others to support that vision.

LEAD FROM WITHIN

Implementing innovative solutions takes leadership. Innovative solutions require a change in perspective and a change in thinking. Sales leaders champion those changes for the customer within their own organizations.

You would think that everyone in the organization would welcome a chance to accommodate customer requirements or new ways of serving them, but there will always be some who resist. They will argue that the organization doesn't do what you are proposing. They will argue that it will cost too much, that it isn't in the budget, and that if they do what you want it will mean they can't do something else. They will suggest that it will not work. They will stand behind protocol.

I've observed that in many cases, the most difficult part of the sale or of implementing the sale isn't getting the customer to agree—it is getting the support of people inside your own company to do what needs to be done, or to do it quickly enough that you don't lose your credibility with the customer or your competitive position. Many times it is the classic battle between sales and marketing or product management.

As a leader, you want to be prepared to communicate your vision for the customer solution clearly, compellingly, persistently, and patiently to win the support of these internal people. You want to convey to them that although what you are proposing may seem different, difficult, or even impossible, all need to keep in mind that they work for the customer. If you need support that is out of the ordinary or very different, let people know that most great things are viewed as impossible when first proposed, but come to be accepted as necessary once people get used to them. (How many of us could live without ATMs if they suddenly disappeared?)

In order to get people aligned behind your idea, you will need to take the initiative. You'll need to positively influence your colleagues in your organization to get them to do what you see as needing to be done and do it in a constructive way, not burning bridges. What this means is that rather than forcing support, you work to gain commitment. You can force support, but that will work only so many times before people say no. In essence, you need to "sell" your idea on the inside even more effectively than you sell it on the outside. How do you do this? By being a leader.

Peggy Champlin, formerly an engineering manager with a Canadian technology supplier, saw firsthand the challenges of getting engineering and marketing and sales to work together to develop updated or new applications for customers.

> *Engineering is quick to say no. Marketing is eager to say yes. Each had different incentives for their work efforts, and those different incentives could easily cause them to lose sight of whom they were both working for. Marketing saw the sale being at risk and was rewarded for making sales. Engineering had schedule and quality requirements for which they were accountable. With lead times of six to nine months, we had to coordinate all our projects.*
>
> *The salespeople who were the easiest to work with did two things: They respected the constraints we had to work under. And they listened to me—they tried to understand what was possible and what wasn't. I would always try to bend over backward to help them, explaining what we could or could not do. The key was when they were willing to work with me to find ways together to make the customer happy, when they took the technical requirements into account and worked with us to develop the best solution for the customer, given the technology, the schedule, and budgets, and when they did it without an attitude. The leaders knew there were better ways to achieve their goals, to get us working with them. They looked at things from a higher plane.*

Sales Leaders Influence Others

Sales leaders are in the business of influencing others. That includes customers and colleagues (engineers, service, support, or executives) as well. What do people do who are effective at influencing others?

Let's understand the concept of influence by taking a look at how leadership has helped you be successful or how someone in a leadership position has influenced you. Two questions follow that will help you understand the way leaders work. Take a moment to read the exercise and think of a situation that fits. Choose *one* of the two questions.

- Think of a leadership success you've had at any time in your sales career. (This should be an experience where something positive happened in a challenging situation to deliver a solution to a customer as a result of your influence.)
- Go back to a defining moment, a time when you were influenced to follow someone else's lead in a sales initiative that resulted in an innovative approach for solving a customer problem.

Once you have chosen a question, answer these questions as you recall the experience:

- What insights do you have about sales leaders based on your own examples?
- What were the leadership qualities that allowed you to be successful?

When we think about people who have influenced us as leaders or times when we have used our leadership abilities, we associate those times with positive emotions. They are memorable for us and sometimes they positively change the course of our companies, our careers, our lives, or the lives of others. We may not have a lot of these experiences. We would be fortunate if we did. But the times we experience leadership do stand out.

I have a page on my website, salesleaders.com, where I ask people, "Do you know someone who you consider to be a sales leader? If so, what qualities would you say contribute to that person being a sales leader?" I started with my own list and then received a number of additions. I began with some important qualities: integrity/honesty, competency, enthusiasm, vision, energy, empathy, and communication skills. I received suggestions to add the following qualities: motivational and passionate, committed, and servant attitude.

Determining which leadership qualities you possess can give you insights about where your strengths are and where you could improve. Every sales leader will not possess every quality. But each will use those that are necessary and will compensate for those that are weaker.

I have a ten-point sales assessment that I use to help individuals and organizations determine their strengths and areas for improvement. Sales leaders tend to like this type of feedback because it helps them understand themselves better and more objectively.

One of the pitfalls that can happen when you propose innovative solutions is making bad decisions. Avoid framing the problem and the decision in the wrong way from the outset.

Make Better Decisions

Most people don't pay attention to the emotions at play behind the decisions they make, but they can certainly be influential. These emotions can be as simple as what we like or dislike or what we are predisposed to be for or against. Making better decisions depends on developing better decision-making processes.

In a technologically driven company that bid on large contracts, I was asked to examine a competitive situation where this company had lost out on a multimillion-dollar contract. I interviewed key people involved and facilitated a discussion of the case. The case study laid out three phases of the bidding process: the decision to bid, the bid preparation, and the debriefing after the bid was rejected.

I identified several key findings. In particular, it became apparent that the team that was responsible for putting the bid together had locked into a particular approach early on. This approach involved the technology they were planning to propose, the risk they were willing to accept in determining profit or loss should they win the project, and the other companies they were partnering with.

As the bid developed, it was difficult to adjust the approach they had taken and the assumptions they had made. One of the key findings was that instead of locking into a fixed set of assumptions when developing a competitive bid, this organization (and any others in similar situations) should have used a process called *scenario planning*. Scenario planning was first developed by Royal Dutch Shell in the 1970s as a way of trying to decide on major future investments in oil exploration and development. They realized that they couldn't predict the future, and that any single prediction of the future or the assumptions that it was based on could quickly become obsolete and undermine their decision.

Shell decided they needed to examine a range of options. They wanted to provide flexibility to adjust their actions depending on how the world energy and petroleum situations developed. At the time, they weren't sure whether there was going to be an excess of capacity or a shortage. As it turned out, there was a shortage to the extent that the U.S. had gas rationing for a time. By not locking into one prediction of the future, they were able to adjust their approach to take advantage of the evolving situation.

Innovative, large sales involve longer time frames. These longer time frames make it more difficult to predict what will happen within the industry, the client organization, or the financial situation. Having several possible options under consideration makes it easier to change direction and prevail over competitors who have locked themselves into an inflexible course of action.

The key in scenario planning is developing and testing the assumptions that underlie the decision. All too often, these assumptions are not explicitly identified, examined, and critiqued. They may not even be universally understood by the sales team, and the client may be operating under a totally different mind-set. To prevent a major misalignment, you should explicitly discuss, agree on, and write down assumptions. (To do so, you may want to use a technique known as *nominal group*.

This means having people write their own assumptions and collecting them before they hear what others have to say.)

For more information on how Shell developed its scenario planning approach, check their Web site (shell.com). There are a number of examples there of how they have used the process.

Challenging Assumptions

When we make assumptions that turn out not to be true, we can suffer negative consequences. A typical sales example is, "The customer has the budget for what I am proposing" or "I am working with the decision maker." If, in the excitement of going after a sale, you haven't asked the right questions up front (such as assessing budget requirements or the decision process), you may waste a tremendous amount of time. It's better for you to know from the start what you are working with than to find out when you present your recommendation to the customer that your proposal is dead in the water because of existing circumstances that you weren't aware of.

We make assumptions all the time, often based on our experiences. History is replete with examples of outmoded assumptions: the world is flat, no one will break the four-minute mile. To achieve breakthroughs, identify and challenge your own assumptions. Write them down and test them. Don't leave them to chance.

At the very least, identifying and clarifying your assumptions with others will minimize the risk that you and the other person are making *different* assumptions.

To succeed:

- Challenge assumptions.
- Compare with others.
- Create a plan B.

> "Many of us were taught that the cancer cell was so messed up with so many biochemical abnormalities that it was impossible to correct them all and therefore really impossible to kill the cancer cell with medicines that hit specific targets in the cancer cell. The fact is that we know that's

not true. We know that we can get very good responses and perhaps
even cures with very specific targeted molecules. Imagine what we can do
when we start combining them and hitting two or three targets at the
same time."

—Dr. Larry Norton, Memorial Sloan-Kettering Cancer Center,
commenting on the unexpected success of Gleevec, a new
cancer treatment pioneered by Novartis

Success Is Having a Plan B

Here is an example of how having a plan B can make a difference. There
was a machine that played a critical part in making the chip used in cell
phones made by two cell phone manufacturers. The machine was
severely damaged by an electrical surge during a lightning storm.

The team from the company with a plan B went into action, contacting alternative suppliers who were able to ramp up relatively quickly
and begin replacing the production that was lost from the primary facility. While these alternative vendors did not supply as many of the chips
as the primary facility did, they knew the specifications and the process
and could start relatively quickly.

The other company did not have alternative suppliers. They had to
begin to look for them. This was a much more time-consuming process because it meant not only finding the suppliers, but evaluating their
capabilities and then negotiating contracts and other arrangements. It
was reported that this company lost hundreds of millions worth of sales
as a result of this incident when they were not able to produce phones,
all because of one critical machine being damaged. Who do you suppose was the primary beneficiary of these lost sales?

Now imagine if you were the salesperson who could have sold this
account on having a backup.

Either-Or Thinking

Either-or thinking goes right along with wrong or untested assumptions in creating problems for sales professionals. When faced with a
decision, how many times will someone think in terms of only two alter-

natives—"either this or that"—when there may be more possibilities? Don't get caught making that faulty assumption. Also, don't go to extremes without being aware that you are doing it. Going to an extreme eliminates options, and when we eliminate options before we can consider them we end up with suboptimal solutions. People typically go to extremes when they are emotional. (Witness the stock market.)

Get Things Done Right

One of the most critical contributors to your success is the quality of your decisions. Poorly made decisions derail people and projects. Making decisions is part of a leader's life.

Making Tough Decisions

Every leader has to make tough decisions. Tough decisions affect people, involve great uncertainty, or have the potential for significant consequences, both positive and negative. Knowing how *and* when to make tough decisions is a hallmark of decisive leaders. Knowing *what* decisions to make is the trademark of a leader who thinks in long-term outcomes. Make a tough decision prematurely, without considering the facts or the effects, or make it based solely on an emotional overreaction, and it can be a disaster. Put off the decision, procrastinate because of fear, and it can mean missed opportunities or bigger problems. Understanding when to seek counsel and when to move ahead in a business environment that doesn't wait for the *perfect* solution can be the difference between success and second place.

Tough decisions might involve deciding when to go after a sale and how aggressively. Tough decisions could involve deciding how to handle someone who is not fulfilling his or her role on your team. Tough decisions may involve deciding when to stop providing products or services to a customer. Sales leaders don't shy away from the challenges these tough decisions present. These are the kind of decisions they are suited to handling.

Sales Greed

Walking away from a sale is never easy, but if the sale sounds too good to be true it probably is. I had the opportunity to speak with Ken Wheatley, vice president for corporate security for a well-known consumer electronics manufacturer, the president of his own security firm, and a former FBI agent. He related an incident in which a number of well-intentioned salespeople and their companies were duped out of $100 million.

The salespeople involved were led to believe they were going to be able to make a large sale, so they got excited about the possibility—probably too excited. They were told to contact only a certain person, they were given an address in a European country that was supposed to be the company's headquarters but turned out to be a storefront, and they were asked to send samples of products for test evaluation (worth millions—of course, the products were never returned). There were clues that something was amiss, but in the excitement of the promise of large sales, salespeople and others overlooked the clues. It was costly.

Another element of greediness that can slip into the sales process is eagerness to offer financing to win the deal. If the buyer's finances are strong, you won't be risking your company by offering terms. But if the situation deteriorates, your company may be left holding the bag; what seemed like a lucrative sale may turn into an albatross. If highly attractive financing is the *only* reason that the customer is interested in buying, that's a red flag. The sale should stand on its own merits, and financing should be an option for closing it. Otherwise, the real cost of the sale could exceed what the customer is going to pay. Your commission may be based only on the revenue from the sale, but your job may hinge on whether the customer pays.

Make Informed Decisions

Think carefully about the questions you or someone else will need to answer to make an informed decision. Write those questions down. They will be the start of a plan to help you make a timely, quality decision.

Do the research you need to do to answer the questions. Develop supporting data. The more significant the decision, the more carefully you will need to research. If the decision is irreversible, it clearly requires more consideration. If the decision is reversible but would be costly to reverse, give it more consideration. If the decision has the possibility of high impact (on members, employees, revenues, and so on), give it more consideration.

Start with internal resources. Use historical data, forecasts, and colleague review. Use outside resources as needed: the Internet, a library, and a local college can help you find facts, data, stories, and examples.

Get information that supports a rational decision while paying attention to the intuitive sense you have about the decision. That intuitive sense will be based on your experience. Your emotions will certainly influence you. Be sure to understand the extent to which they do. Don't overreact based on past experience.

Gather information methodically but quickly. Develop a plan for gathering the information. Are you the sole person responsible for making the decision? Will you need to present the information to someone else or to a committee? Will the decision be made by consensus?

The more knowledgeable you are, the more confidence you will have in the decision you make. Be open to new options, rather than automatically staying with the status quo.

Don't put off making the decision once you have sufficient information. Take a calculated risk. There is no perfect decision.

> *"Being comfortable with 80 percent of the information and making the decision on time is better than having 100 percent of the information and making the decision late."*
> —Vance Coffman, chairman and CEO, Lockheed Martin

Do It Wholeheartedly or Don't Do It

As soon as you have agreed to do something for someone, that person believes you will do it. You need to demonstrate that you are doing your best to meet that expectation. Not letting him or her down becomes a matter of integrity.

Use Smart Planning

When you have a strong sales team in place, getting everyone on the same page becomes paramount. Most salespeople and their managers are well versed in the goal-setting process, so the following ideas may be a way to refine what you do, especially when you are involved with a more complex project or something out of the ordinary.

Specificity

I did some work with a group that specialized in software for a certain industry. Their goal was to deliver bug-free software to their customers. When I asked how they defined a bug, they spent at least fifteen minutes debating it. Some people argued that it was a malfunction in the coding, which is what I think most people would say is a bug. But some said the malfunction could be due to a misinterpretation of the client's requirements. Others said it could mean that the documentation for the software was incorrect, misleading, or difficult to follow. What the customers wanted was software that worked right the first time and every time. They probably also wanted it to be easy to use and consistent. So if you widen the scope of the idea of a "bug," you could see how it might look from the customer's point of view.

Regardless of what anyone said, it was clear that there was no commonly agreed-to definition of what a bug was—and if they weren't sure what a bug was, how could they be sure that they were delivering bug-free software?

What seemed self-evident to everyone became uncertain as the discussion progressed. That was actually good because it gave them a chance to reexamine this goal to make sure they knew what it really meant, not just to them but also to their customers.

All too often, the problem with goals is that people think they know what they are supposed to achieve, but their objectives are not specific enough. When asked to describe what result they really are expected to achieve, it becomes apparent that it is ambiguous.

I use an example in some of my workshops where I offer to paint the inside of someone's home. Usually, someone will accept my offer. The person will be interested until I describe how I will paint the interior of their home. They almost always say, "No thanks." What started out to be a simple goal, painting the inside of their home, turns out to be something very different from what they envisioned. The problem is that the goal wasn't specific enough to begin with.

There are two ways to measure success in reaching goals: objectively or subjectively. When you set sales goals, you typically set them based on objective measurements: number of units or revenue, for example. You may also look at objectives for retaining customers or obtaining new customers or certain types of new customers. Counting the number of units tallies objective measurements.

Subjective measurements are a matter of opinion. One of the most important subjective measurements for salespeople is customer satisfaction. Whether the customers are happy about the service they are getting is a matter of individual perception—completely subjective. We run into subjective measurements every day. Someone will say, "On a scale from one to ten, where ten is greatest or best, where would you say you are right now?" Or customers are asked to indicate whether they are highly satisfied, satisfied, neither satisfied nor dissatisfied, dissatisfied, or highly dissatisfied.

Some people prefer to deal in hard numbers, but keep in mind that important decisions that customers make are based on their subjective opinions. They like something or they don't like it. Understanding their opinions becomes crucial to providing the solutions they want in the way they want them and retaining them as customers. To have a balanced picture of your success, look at both objective and subjective measurements of success.

"Stretch" Objectives

I have a quick exercise I ask people to do in my workshops when we talk about setting objectives. The exercise involves stretching beyond where they thought they could stretch. In asking tens of thousands of people to do this exercise, I have rarely found someone who couldn't do a bit more than what they thought they could do. The point with the exercise is that we sometimes place constraints on ourselves that aren't there and that when we think creatively about what we have to do we can find ways to accomplish ten times as much. When we work with others together as a team, there is just about nothing that we can't accomplish given the resources.

If you find yourself too often in a crisis mode trying to meet deadlines, the following discussion is one of the most useful ways of getting out of that way of working. There are three types of time frames inherent in meeting deadlines. The first type is the most common: the deadline, when the objective or project is scheduled to be met or completed. The second type of time frame is the milestones, the intermediate dates that must be met if the deadline is going to be met. The third type of time frame is the start date. The problem with focusing on the due date is that it is far into the future. Today, if I am fighting the crisis of the day, I say to myself, "I know that project is due, but it's not due until next month. I'll start it tomorrow." Of course, when tomorrow rolls around, what happens? I have another crisis. When do I actually start that project? When it's due, because now it's a crisis. What should you do instead? Focus on the start date, when the project or task must be started if it is going to be finished on time. What does that change in focus do? It gives the start date a sense of urgency that helps it compete with the crises and interruptions. They are urgent, but will not necessarily contribute value.

It's beneficial to focus on the start date and milestones. When someone starts to distract you away from the project you are working on, you can explain that you have a deadline to meet, and it's true. You know that if you don't meet the immediate deadline you won't meet the final one. People will usually accept this explanation. This helps you control interruptions and get work done on time.

Quantity answers the question "How much?" or "How many?" This is typically the easiest part to specify. Quality answers the question "How well?" This is often the most difficult part to specify, but it is the most important because it usually makes the biggest impression on the customer, who defines quality. You don't want to be surprised. If you are ever given a choice about delivering a result on time but of questionable quality versus delivering something late of unquestionable quality, opt for delivering the quality product that meets expectations. Earl Nightingale said that people remember the quality of what we deliver long after they've forgotten when we delivered it. Without a doubt, it's best to meet a schedule, but if you can't meet a schedule, keep the customer informed.

The most difficult part of specifying a goal is describing what you want when the job is done. I was working on a project one time and got to a point where I needed direction from the person who had asked me to do the project, something more specific about what he was looking for. I said, "I'm not sure what you're looking for." He said, "I'm not sure either, but I'll know it when I see it." That meant I was going to have to waste a lot of time spinning my wheels to come up with a variety of approaches until he saw one he liked.

Time specifies when the objective must be met. Again, time is usually not a major issue, except as it relates to procrastination.

Have a Plan

Some people are reluctant to plan because circumstances can change so quickly, potentially making well-laid plans obsolete. The problem is that you don't have the time *not* to plan. You don't have the luxury of wasting time, and that is what you end up doing if you don't plan. A sales professional who goes into a customer meeting without careful planning is going to waste time and opportunity. The sales professional needs at least a clear objective and an agenda for the meeting. He or she also needs to do homework to find out as much as possible ahead of time about the customer, the company, and its preferred ways of working. The sales professional also needs to be prepared to ask or answer questions or to make a convincing presentation.

For example, planning could include doing something as straightforward as making a sales call on the telephone. Do you have an objective for the call? How long do you expect the call to take? How will you proceed with the call? Make sure it is as short as possible while covering everything you need to cover.

Once you hang up, if you've forgotten an important point you wanted to cover, you know how difficult it can be to get the person back on the phone again or how time consuming voice mail is.

One sales manager complained to me about some salespeople who worked for him and didn't plan the rambling messages they left for him. He said he once thought a message was over and started to hang up when he heard, "Oh, by the way . . ." but it was too late. The manager had already hung up. He would have preferred the salespeople to start the call by saying, "I have three things I need to cover," and then go through them quickly.

Many of the salespeople comment after they complete one of my workshops that they realize the importance of planning. It's easy to understand. Salespeople tend to be action oriented, to want to get started and get things done. So when I do a workshop that shows the benefits of planning, from the perspective of being better able to quickly win customers' trust and identify their concerns, they see the payoff in precall planning and other planning activities.

When I have worked with people on developing plans, most of the time they think of their experience with corporate plans—long, involved, and not used. A plan can be as uncomplicated as you would like and can be done on a page. When Jack Welch was an up-and-coming CEO at GE, he said he resented the long plans he had been asked to put together because he didn't think they had value. When he became CEO, he changed the way the divisional plans were presented so that the key elements could be shown on a single page.

The easiest way to think of planning is to think of it as answering the question "How?" Goals and objectives answer the question "What?" What is it you want to achieve? Purpose answers the question "Why?" Why are we doing this? Why are we in business? Why are we having this meeting?

Of these three questions, "Why?" is the most important. People want to understand why they are doing something. If they are only told what to do, they feel there is something missing. When people are not told why they are doing something, they can feel as if they are there to do and not to think. If people have a good enough reason, a compelling "why" to do something, they will figure out the how.

Planning addresses the how. How will we achieve our goals? How will we complete this project on time and with the quality that it is supposed to have? How will we know that we have been successful?

Planning is filling in the steps between where you are and where you want to go. It breaks down the process into a series of steps. In project management we call this a *work breakdown structure*. You might have heard or worked with GANTT charts. GANTT charts show the steps in a project and the timelines for meeting each of them. They are a much easier way to present a schedule than the standard list of tasks and dates. A sample GANTT chart is shown in figure 8.

One of the key things I've learned from working on projects is that not only do you have to back up from the implementation or completion date if you're going to meet customer deadlines, you must communicate with customers about how important it is for them to make timely decisions if you're going to be able to *meet* their time requirements.

I worked with a client on a customized program for a national sales meeting. The program was scheduled over four months from the time when we first spoke, but by the time they evaluated the proposal, made

Figure 8

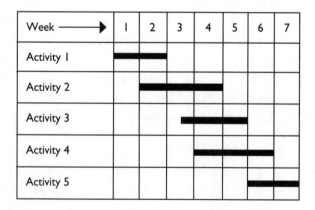

a decision to go ahead, signed the agreement, and sent the deposit, there was barely a month left for development. We were still able to develop the program content as agreed, but it was too close.

What I realized from working with this client was that I needed to inform the client about the timeline for meeting their requirements. They probably felt they had plenty of time in which to make a decision, and I didn't think at first that it was going to take so long for them to make it. In the future, on a longer-lead project such as this one I will communicate with the client about what needs to be done by when so they have a clear sense of what we need to do to move ahead and meet their requirements in a quality way. A simple timeline that shows key decision points, starting from the implementation date and working back, is a good way to communicate this. It can be a GANTT chart for more complex projects, or just a single timeline for less involved ones. Either will work.

Some of the main elements that a plan should include are shown in the planning template on the next page.

Ten Reasons People Don't Achieve Their Goals
- *Unclear goals:* You can't do what you can't describe.
- *Too many goals at one time:* This makes it difficult to concentrate on one long enough to get it done.
- *A lack of priorities:* Time is wasted on less important goals first.
- *Conflicting goals:* Working on one goal creates problems for another (for example, quantity versus quality).
- *A lack of resources:* You don't have enough time, money, people, equipment, or training.
- *A lack of specific action plans:* This is design without implementation.
- *A lack of belief in the goal or the ability to achieve it:* Failure becomes a self-fulfilling prophecy.
- *A lack of focus:* This can cause jumping from one goal to another.
- *A lack of follow-through:* Some people start well but give up too soon.
- *Missing accountability:* No consequences exist when people do not follow through.

A ONE-PAGE PLANNING TEMPLATE

Goal/objective (for example, delivery of a specific product or service)

Purpose (meeting customer commitment)

Expected outcomes/results (for example, revenue, customer satisfaction, referrals)

Measurements

    Critical success factors

    Quantity

    Quality criteria

    Time

    Start date

    End date

Resources (budgeting and people)

Training/support required

Technology constraints

Responsibilities

Contingencies

Are any of these obstacles getting in your way? If so, which are most troublesome?

Remember to keep your written goals visible. Out of sight, out of mind.

Set Your Sights High

If you are going to set your sights, why *not* set them high? If you get what you set your sights on, why not get what you want? If you set them high and don't get what you want, you may be disappointed. But better to be disappointed than to miss an opportunity that you may never have again.

Follow the lead of the people who are leaders higher in the organization and who model the type of behavior you would like to develop— the type of behavior that gets things done through effective communication and relationships. Watch what they get involved with and how they achieve their goals. Emulate their way of working and then adapt it so that it works best for you.

The Next Level

What is your plan for taking your business, your sales, your products or services, and your knowledge and skills to the next level? What is the next level for you? This is a question every sales leader must answer. Growth takes planning. Sustainable growth takes planning for several steps.

When you start to think about what that next level might look like, consider the following:

- The greatest challenge facing you in sales
- The most significant change you can anticipate
- An area in which you could make a quantum improvement

From Mystery to Mastery

If you tend not to move ahead to do something because you aren't sure what to do, it's easy to procrastinate. Instead, remove the mystery. Learn what you need to learn or do what you need to do so that the mystery is gone. When scientists set out to find a cure for a disease, they don't know exactly what they have to do, so they may try many approaches in order to learn what works and what doesn't. As they narrow their search, they learn in depth about a particular strategy. *Answers become clear only through action.*

When you don't know something, it has an element of mystery about it. If you remove the mystery, your knowledge increases, and with that your confidence. When your confidence increases you will be more likely to move ahead. When you move ahead, you gain invaluable experience, further increasing your knowledge and mastery, further increasing your confidence. When you master a subject or a skill, you know it extremely well. Become a master of your craft.

> *"If you want to accomplish twice as much as your competition, you must work twice as hard."*
>
> —Wayne Huizenga, chairman of Republic Industries, Inc.,
> former chairman of Blockbuster Entertainment, and
> cofounder of Waste Management Inc.

The Core of Law 6: Lead from Within

Sales leaders lead their proposed customer solution, supported by sound decisions, through their own organization.

MAKE IT A TEAM EFFORT

Consider the following comments from sales professionals: "My biggest frustration is that, due to our internal processes, I spend longer negotiating with different departments within the company to get things done than with customers to get more sales."

"Over the last couple of years with this company, my biggest challenge has been to find my place and role within a new sales team and to get accepted by other members of the team as a valuable player and by customers as a valuable ally."

It takes teamwork to deliver high-value, innovative solutions. Whether that involves team selling or the team behind the scenes, to deliver on time and on target requires more than just the effort of the salesperson. The salesperson can't and shouldn't do it all.

A team shares a common *goal* or *purpose* and must work *together* to achieve it. Having a team is the starting point. To be an effective leader, you need to be supported by a high-performing team.

- A high-performing team communicates effectively.
- A high-performing team reaches better decisions.
- A high-performing team exceeds expectations.

In what ways do you need the support of a team to deliver reliable services for your customers? Are there times when establishing a high-performance team is a challenge for you?

The *Wall Street Journal* reported that one of the most successful pharmaceutical companies had taken "aggressive" steps to upgrade its sales force. Collaboration, the ability to work effectively with others, was one of the key attributes of its best salespeople and one that it looks for in new hires. Your ability to work effectively as a team member and to lead that team when needed will play a large part in determining how successful you will be. There are limited opportunities today where a salesperson can operate as a "lone ranger." People skills, not only sales or technical skills, help top producers get things done.

Your team may consist of you and a technical support person, such as a sales engineer. It may consist of you and the people responsible for product development. It may consist of you and the people who are responsible for implementation or service. While you may not work closely with all of these people all of the time, any one of them can help you make this sale and the next one.

Unfortunately, when you or the people who must support you in delivering correct solutions on time don't see themselves as working on your team, you are going to take a lot longer to do what you need to do and may not even be able to get it done. You need to overcome any tendencies among people or departments to work at cross purposes. Create a sense of commitment to a common goal or purpose that centers on your customer's requirements and satisfaction. Your ability to do this is highly dependent on your ability to communicate and to balance your own ego with the needs of the people on your team.

In communicating with your support team, especially when something has gone wrong, it is critical that you control your response and be careful not to say something you'll regret. Channel your response into preventing future problems. Be the model. Know that you are constantly on stage and being evaluated and emulated.

The four cornerstones of successful teams are four opportunities to develop that sense of commitment.

Four Cornerstones of Successful Sales Teams

The foundation of successful sales teams consists of four cornerstones:

- A common goal or purpose
- Good communication

- Team development
- Team attitude

A team must share a common purpose or goal to be a team. A sales leader often must work to gain the support of people who work behind the scenes. This might include product development, delivery, service, engineering, and support staff. It may involve working with other vendors. It may involve working with people who are going to run your sale through the design, development, implementation, or billing process. In any case, everyone on that team must work together to realize the goal.

Good communication flows in all directions in a timely and effective way. Team members know what is expected, they know how they are doing, and they know about customer changes before customers know about the changes.

Team development means that the team develops its ability to work together as a team. High-performing teams don't leave this to chance. They don't spend inordinate time doing this, but they also don't ignore it. They know that to deliver the solutions they promise to customers, they need to rely on people in support positions, in engineering, in information processing, in billing, in customer service, and in other parts of the company. Sales leaders take the time to ensure that people on their team are clear on what the team needs to accomplish, feel they are being heard, are glad to be a part of the team, and recognize the efforts of the individual team members who contribute to the team's success.

Your team development efforts might consist of having a meeting (or a series of meetings) with the people on your team. The meetings can have a number of purposes:

- Communicating customer needs
- Seeking others' input or understanding others' concerns
- Examining resources and finding solutions to problems
- Gaining the commitment of team members to goals
- Coming to agreement on priorities and next steps

Team attitude means that when people on the team care about the customers and about helping each other, the team is going to find ways around problems. They will fill in for each other as needed. They will be proactive and head off problems. They will step up as individuals and assume leadership roles as needed to meet the team's commitments. As team members, they take their team commitments seriously. They consider their other team members to be their customers. They minimize hidden agendas, and although they may have allegiances to the departments or people they work for, they keep communication open, and once they make a commitment they follow through on it.

Each of these team components plays a role in the team's success. In smaller proposals, the team's attitude may be the single most important determinant of success. The team may be working with limited resources in short time frames. Communication will normally flow more easily if the group is smaller. Team development may involve one, or at most two, startup meetings to identify roles and outline how the team will work together.

In projects involving larger proposals, these elements become more significant. The team's goal must be absolutely clear; communication must flow freely and be comprehensive and timely; and the team needs to think about how it works together. Attitude will play a role and will normally be a positive factor when people are excited about the challenge ahead.

Develop Commitment with Others

The difference between commitment and compliance is the difference between *want* to and *have* to. All of us have been in a position where we were told to do something. Most times, we do it without resisting because it is a part of every job. But when you are told to do something important that will take a great deal of effort and don't fully understand why, you will do it because you have to, but your level of commitment won't be as high as it would be if you understood why it was necessary and believed that your ideas were valued. In that case you would have a higher level of commitment to the project.

You probably have seen that when people are compliant, they do what they need to do to get by. They may not put forth any extra effort. If you've been on a team that has a high level of commitment, you know how exciting it can be and how much each person will do to make sure the project is successful.

If you depict the level of commitment as a spectrum, you can visualize how different degrees of commitment are possible (see figure 9).

Top sales professionals must influence others in their organizations in order to do what they promised the customer they would do. Exceptional sales professionals are able to win commitment from others. How do they do that?

One way is to explain the "why"—that is, the purpose or benefit to the customer of what you would like to do. How will it help or affect the person whose support you need? This gives people a sense of the big picture and a reason to be committed. Ask for and consider their ideas. People are more committed to their own ideas than to those of others. If you can't use their ideas, at least explain why not. Recognize their efforts when they achieve the objective. Without recognition, people won't extend themselves the next time.

These steps, when carried out with genuine interest in the input and success of the people you work with, are more likely to lead to their support. If you are the person initiating the change, consider product management, engineering, or support staff to be *your* customers. Do your homework to find out what *their* needs and concerns are before you present them with requests, and you will find it a lot easier to make a "sale." Be very careful to demand what you want. People may give you what you demand, but you may find it to be less than what you need.

Figure 9

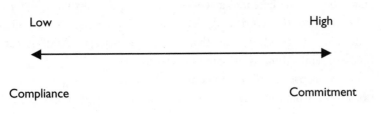

Recognize People's Efforts

The idea behind recognition is pretty simple. People want to be sincerely appreciated for their efforts and accomplishments. When they are, they tend to want to help you even more. When they are not outwardly appreciated but aren't criticized, they will do what they need to do to get their jobs done, but may not extend themselves beyond that. If they are inappropriately criticized for what they do, they will tend to do the least they can do to get by and will spend a lot of time commiserating with each other about how much they dislike the way they are treated.

Offer Constructive Feedback

From time to time, you're going to find you need to let someone who supports you know that he or she needs to do something differently. How you say it will be critical to the response you get. Offering constructive feedback is one of the most important ways that you can influence others positively. It can mean the difference between getting what you want and getting nothing.

If I said to you, "That was a great recommendation, but it was too long," it sounds good to you until I get to the word "but." As soon as you hear that, don't you find yourself tensing up? Don't you suspect that I'm just getting ready to say what I *really* wanted to say?

If I said, "That was a great recommendation, and if you can get it into just one page, which we can use as an overview for the customer, it will be close to perfect," wouldn't that sound a lot better? The key is to change the word "but" to the word "and."

"But" is negative. As soon as you say "but," you negate any positive statement that preceded it. If the recommendation was 95 percent good, "but" focuses the listener's attention on the 5 percent that wasn't good. When you use the word "and," it is additive. You recognize the 95 percent that was good and say that you can add to it. "And" is future focused, while "but" is oriented toward the past.

All of us use "but" in the context of trying to give people suggestions about what they can do to improve. It is a strongly ingrained habit.

Give yourself time to start remembering not to use the word "but" after you've told someone something positive.

A number of years ago I was on the telephone after I had finished a speech. A fellow who had been in the audience was standing next to me. I was on hold, so I couldn't help but overhear what he was saying. He was talking to someone at work. He said something like, "I'm glad you were able to get that out on time, but you should have . . ." He stopped at that point and said, "I'm not supposed to use the word 'but.' Let me start over." Most of us will find that it will take a bit of undoing to start using the word "and" in these situations. (By the way, "however" is the same as the word "but," just a little milder.)

A lot of times people want to give others feedback about how to improve. They rely on the cookie-sandwich approach, which has been suggested for many years as a way to give feedback: start with the good news, give the bad news, and finish up on a positive note. It is much more productive to avoid the "bad news" tone by using "and" instead of "but."

If you need to give someone corrective feedback and the person is not producing a result that is acceptable, communicate that point directly and diplomatically. Just say something like, "There's a problem with such-and-such. I need to sit down and talk with you about it."

Always keep in mind that your tone of voice in all of these interactions says a great deal. "What do you think?" can be said with many different tones of voice. How it comes across will depend on what you intend to convey. If you expect the person to respond positively, communicate that in your tone of voice. Be in control of the interaction.

Avoid the Temptation to Say . . .

All of us are tempted from time to time to say it when we are right and someone else is wrong: "I told you so." Instead, empathize, don't criticize. Have you ever misjudged someone? Have you ever misinterpreted someone else's behavior? Have you ever made a mistake? Can you remember how easily it happened? Can you recall how quickly you realized what had happened?

Then you can put yourself in others' shoes and try to understand rather than judge, empathize rather than criticize. You will be more objective and more likely to reach an understanding. Great salespeople and great leaders are able to be empathic. They create high levels of trust and understanding that are the foundations of effective and productive relationships.

Zig Ziglar, CPAE, has advice that is extremely helpful in these situations: never try to top the customer. If the customer tells you how bad or good something is or about something that happened to him or her, don't tell your own story that shows you had it worse or better. If you do, the customer will feel you are competing. Don't even try to match the customer with your own story. Instead, listen, laugh, or empathize with his or her situation, and he or she will know you are listening.

Delegate and Deliver

Top producers delegate. They have to. They know that they need to concentrate on the most critical customer activities, the ones for which they are most uniquely qualified. Top producers know they can't get it all done themselves and still be top producers. You can delegate tasks to an assistant, to other professionals, or to a team. The bigger the sales you work on, the more you need to delegate. If you work by yourself, you will limit how much you can sell. If your vision is to grow your sales as if it were for your own business, treat it as if it were your own business. A Fortune 500 company couldn't run if the CEO tried to do everything. The only limit to your growth is how big your dream is and how effectively you enlist others to help you reach it. Don't get stuck in the mundane. It won't help you achieve greatness.

Answer yes or no to each of the following questions to get a quick assessment of your attitude toward delegation.

- Do you ever find yourself doing work that someone else could or should do?
- Do you ever find yourself doing work rather than taking the time to explain it to someone else?

- Do you ever do work that should be done by someone else because you want to make sure it's done correctly?

If you answered yes to two or three of these questions, you could become more productive by delegating more. You might immediately think, "But no one works for me. I don't have anyone to delegate to." In this age when salespeople often work without any assigned office administrators, that is a legitimate concern. But there are alternatives.

An example of an opportunity for delegation came up as I prepared a presentation for a client's national sales meeting. One of the salespeople I interviewed said that when a customer call came in for a quote on a specific service, he would calculate the pricing himself rather than passing that call to the service people. Calculating the pricing wasn't something he needed to do. Once the account had been won, the service people could handle specific orders. Winning the account was his job. Of course, keeping it was his job also, which is where some of the uncertainty arose about when he should or should not help serve the customer.

There were several reasons he calculated pricing for the customer on a specific service. First, he wanted to make sure the pricing was correct. Second, he didn't want the customer to feel slighted. Third, helping this customer was something that was easy to do, easier than going out to face rejection—a form of procrastination. Unfortunately, while he was in the office helping this customer he wasn't out developing new business. If this were an isolated case it wouldn't matter. But when it happens several times or repeatedly, it means that this salesperson is not doing what he should be doing. He was doing someone else's job.

If he were to pass the call to a service person, his way of explaining this delegation to the customer would be critical in maintaining the customer's trust. The best way to handle situations such as these is to make sure customers are aware of the possibilities in advance. Once the account has been won, the salesperson can let the customer know that the service people will be helping him with specific pricing questions in the future.

The best way to convince customers that this is the best course of action is to tell them the benefits of doing it the way you are suggesting and explaining why it is in their best interests. (Typically, if they save time or avoid communication or technical errors, they will willingly accept the explanation.) You could say something such as, "I very much appreciate your business. I am going to go over your account with my service people, who have the expertise to help quickly and accurately with the specific pricing on each service. They also will help you if something comes up that you didn't anticipate. I will be staying in touch with you to make sure that we are providing service to your satisfaction and to see what new services may be of benefit to you. And, of course, you can always call me if there is any problem that you feel you aren't getting resolved through them. Does that sound like a good approach to you?"

Alternatively, if the salesperson didn't alert the customer about this arrangement in advance, the first time the customer calls in with a request the salesperson could get the service person on the line at the same time with the customer, introduce the customer to the service person, and have the service person either figure out the pricing with the salesperson on the line (if there is anything unusual about it) or have the service person speak directly with the customer. In either case, the customer gets the help he or she needs and the salesperson can use that time to go find other customers to help. Obviously, you don't want customers to feel as if you are putting them off, but to know that you want them to get the best service possible.

Delegation doesn't have to be all or nothing. That's the kind of thinking that prevents people from considering delegation in the first place.

Why don't salespeople delegate? First, they don't think they can because they don't have anyone working for them. But they can ask service and marketing people to do what they are supposed to do, when they are supposed to do it. In this way, the salesperson can do what he or she is supposed to do: sell.

Second, they may be afraid that they will be held accountable if they delegate a high-profile task to someone who doesn't do it right. That's a reasonable fear. But they also believe that if they are held accountable they will suffer dire consequences, such as a loss of prestige, responsibility, and possibly a job. They take it to an extreme and see themselves on the street and jobless because they delegated this one assignment. This may not be rational, but fears are often irrational.

So what should you do when you delegate? Here are three important steps.

- Prepare the person you will delegate to. If needed, get the person the correct information about the current products or services the customer has.
- Be clear with the person about what the boundaries are to that authority. For example, do you want the service person to call the customer directly and inform you?
- Be certain to agree with the person about what will be done and when. (Customers' calls will be returned within twenty-four hours, for example.)

Returning to our example, if the salesperson is unsure that the service people will be able to handle the pricing, he could meet with them when an account is won and go over any special arrangements they need to be aware of. If the service person was new, the salesperson could ask the service person to let him review any pricing on the first occasion or two or when specific circumstances arise. The salesperson could follow up with the service person and review the account periodically to ensure that the pricing is being handled correctly and to see whether there are trends or patterns in the customer's purchases that he should be aware of. In this way, the salesperson has assurance that the customer is getting the right pricing and service while also leveraging his time to work with other customers. He can introduce the customer to services that the customer could take advantage of. That creates a win-win outcome.

The less time you spend on service, the more time you can spend developing business and selling. That's the benefit of delegating.

Micromanaging Is Tempting, Time Consuming, and Ineffective

Have you ever been micromanaged? Have you ever felt you had to micromanage someone else? In either case, it is not a positive experience. How does this come about? What can you do to prevent it? What are the alternatives?

There are several reasons that people start to micromanage. They micromanage when they concentrate on activities instead of results, when they observe what people do instead of measuring what they accomplish. This problem often is rooted in the goal-setting process, when goals aren't clear, specific, or realistic, or aren't set at all.

Regardless of how someone comes to the point of micromanaging, it isn't good and it shouldn't continue. It should instead be replaced with a results-oriented goal-setting process and measurement of progress at preagreed milestones. Couple those actions with positive reinforcement of accomplishments and over time you won't need to micromanage someone.

Instead of thinking that you have to manage someone, think about how you need to communicate with that person. Think about how to make sure you and that person share the same understanding about what has to be done and why. Also, think about how you can influence this person to want to do what has to be done with the best possible quality. Think about how you will seek to understand the concerns and requirements that this person has. Anticipate how you will respond to his or her ideas and suggestions.

You don't need to make all the decisions. Just be aware of when you need to be involved and when it is better to not oversee work.

The three keys to avoiding micromanaging your sales efforts are to:

- Get agreement on the specific results you expect, when they will be ready, and how you will measure their quality.
- Build in checkpoints at agreed-upon milestones.
- Make sure everyone has the resources and skills needed to do the job.

When you are working with someone who is relatively new, you may need to ensure more oversight at first, which may mean more frequent checkpoints. When you work with someone who is experienced, give more autonomy but always maintain good communication with that person; if you find more direction is needed, you can always give it. Approach this in a relaxed yet focused manner and other people will be more receptive, more relaxed, and more focused. They will reflect your frame of mind. A leader inspires people to do great things. No one manages people to do great things.

When Tom Hanks was filming *Saving Private Ryan*, the cast went through rigorous military training. After enduring this for some time, the cast approached Hanks and said that they had had their fill of it and were going to stop. Hanks called the director, Steven Spielberg, and told him about the situation. Spielberg told him, "You're a leader. Figure it out." Hanks went back to the cast and simply said to them, "If you think you can portray these soldiers the way they *really* were, then go. Otherwise, stay." Everyone stayed.

Sales Leaders Are Communicators

While working with a client, I had been directed to one of their top salespeople as a model for the way they would like their other salespeople to sell. Bob had been instrumental at maintaining an account worth millions of dollars. The customer had been considering shutting down the project this company was running, disappointed in its progress. When I asked Bob what he did to keep the project from being canceled, he replied that he had earned their trust. When he worked with this customer, a multidepartmental account, he devoted a great deal of time to communicating with people. He had multiple points of contact with the account in different departments. When he was with a person in one department discussing a situation and he realized that the person wasn't aware of what was going on in another department, he would say, "I just met with so-and-so yesterday. He said they have come up with another approach on that. Here's what it involves."

He played a role within the organization, that of the eyes and ears that people inside the organization sometimes didn't have the opportunity to play. So when it was time to fight for keeping his company's project on track, people were willing to listen to him. When he acted as this communication link, he wasn't doing it with a specific sale in mind. He was doing it to build the relationship by doing something that was of value to the people in the customer's organization. That was one of the things that made him one of the sales leaders in his organization.

A Minute Is a Long Time

In one of my presentation skills workshops, a banquet manager from the hotel did a short presentation about how long a minute seems to a guest waiting for food to be delivered by room service. He asked the people in the audience to close their eyes and open them when they thought a minute had passed. As you might guess, most people opened their eyes long before the minute was up. We all know how long a minute seems when you are anxiously waiting for something that you expect shortly.

Customers are no different. When they leave a voice message, a page, or an E-mail, they expect a timely reply, even if it is only to say that you got their message and are working on a response. Depending on the urgency of their call, they may get increasingly frustrated with each moment or hour that goes by. They might go over your head to get an answer and then vent their frustration at your company's lack of responsiveness.

Can you think of a time when someone didn't respond to your phone call? How much did you tolerate before you decided that you wouldn't give that company any more of your business? What was your business worth?

Have a backup when you are out of the office, in meetings, or unavailable. Check your messages frequently. Leave an assistant's number. In an account with a strong relationship, they will have multiple contacts at your company. Encourage them to call certain specific people if you aren't available and then ask those other people to let you know when they get a call from a customer. Give your home number to your best customers. But be responsive in their time frame, getting back to them as quickly as they would like, given whatever constraints you have. Apologize when you can't respond as quickly as they might have liked.

Perception

Customers like to be associated with a winner. If it looks like you and your company are on the rise, they will have a more positive feeling about dealing with you. So it is in your best interests, when you communicate with customers or potential customers, that you create a positive and honest perception about the course of your success. Keep your customers informed about events affecting you or your company.

Don't leave communication to chance. Create a plan to enhance your image. Writing articles is a good way to do this. Announcing a big or unusual sale, helping a customer with a difficult situation (with their permission), or participating in community or charitable events are other possible ways to communicate progress.

If you or your company encounter downturns, it is better to communicate and explain the issues to customers (if possible) than to have them read about the problems in the paper. I'm not suggesting you simply put a spin on the event. Instead, help customers understand how this news may affect them.

During one of my marketing assignments at AT&T, we asked a telecommunications manager from one of our major customers to speak to our group. He told us how decisions we had made in the past had made it difficult to manage the budget. As a result, his predecessor had been asked to leave. Because of his admonishment, we set up a communications program with our major customers that worked through account managers. People familiar with our services went to customers to tell them about the general direction of our services so customers could better plan their budgets. Customers liked the information and, I believe, the attention they received. These presentations allowed customers to make more informed decisions. Effective communication helps remove uncertainty and create confidence.

"We Took the Lead"

The Harris Corporation is an international company that provides communication solutions for government and commercial applications. One of its divisions, Harris RF Communications, was instrumental in helping General Dynamics to win a major contract with the United Kingdom (UK) Ministry of Defence, one of the UK's largest programs for modernization of its military communications.

The Harris RF team—led by the pursuit champion, George Helm, and the proposal manager, Chris Aebli—worked as a subcontractor to General Dynamics for the project. The team helped to win one of the most important military communications projects in recent UK history and Harris's largest tactical radio contract ever. And they did it by helping dislodge an in-country, established vendor. How were they able to do it?

"We took the lead among the subcontractors to demonstrate that we could deliver the solution quickly. It was a risk-reduction demonstration to inspire confidence in our company that we would be a low-risk choice," said Aebli. Like most customers, governments want to know that what is promised will be delivered, and when there are billions of dollars at stake they can't afford to be wrong.

Leadership Principles

To win a tough competitive situation where there is an established vendor, it is imperative to start with the right solution. The Harris team knew it had the right solution; their challenge was to prove it. They knew they had to prove their solution had the lowest risk for on-time delivery, with the capabilities the customer wanted, and at a competitive price. That should be a winning combination in any situation, but the contract was far from certain unless the team could demonstrate beyond a doubt that its technology would work, and work better than the competition's. "We knew our biggest risk was incorporating the encryption module from the UK," says Helm. "That's where we figured the competition had the advantage based on an earlier contract they had won for that type of component." What allowed this team to win? Three leadership principles contributed.

First, the team identified the most important concern the customer had about Harris. It made a decision immediately that it would completely satisfy that concern—whether it could provide a working solution on time—through product demonstrations.

Second, the team "sold" the project internally by creating confidence with top management that it could win the bid. This helped get full top management support.

Third, the team made strategic decisions at the beginning about the message it needed to get to the customer.

Military projects such as these go through a bid/no-bid decision within the corporation because there is typically a significant cost in just bidding on the project. So if the decision is made to go ahead and bid, it has to be with the understanding that there is a good chance of winning the contract. In this case, the thinking was, "This was a job we weren't going to lose." That helped set the tone for everything else that followed.

The team decided right from the start that providing impressive product demonstrations early in the selection process was their one opportunity to prove their low-risk solution and, if successful, was key to its ability to strengthen General Dynamics's offer. Key Harris people had been tracking the existing program for a number of years, and before the request for a proposal came out, held a meeting in the UK with the customer. That meeting helped Harris understand what the customer considered to be the "crown jewels" of the program and allowed Harris to reflect on the strengths and weaknesses of its own offer.

Establishing the Team

This was a huge opportunity for Harris, and nothing quite like it had been undertaken before. One challenge was to get a massive number of people working on it quickly—the team drew on people they had worked with before. Harris put many of their best people on the problem, gaining time by minimizing the learning curve. They collocated them, took them out of their "regular" jobs and isolated them from distractions. Other key individuals pulled into the program included the director of HF radio engineering and the European sales director. The engineering director led the effort to perform the successful product demonstrations. The director of sales, located in the UK, established the right contacts for all of the in-country meetings and provided a day-to-day contact with General Dynamics's offices throughout the UK.

One of the team's main objectives was to maximize the positive impact they could have on the award decision as a subcontractor. As a result, they knew that communicating their message to the customer was going to be key. The strategy and message were put together at the beginning: eliminate any weakness perceived in the Harris product offering and unquestionably prove, by way of early demonstration, that it had a low-risk offering that met or exceeded the customer's expectations. That preparation gave the organization confidence in the bidding process and gave the team the resources it needed to do the job. Thorough preparation and an attitude that "we have the best product and we're going to prove it" led to a self-fulfilling prophecy.

Creativity Leads to a Fast Response

The team knew they were going up against an established competitor. The prime contractor on the project, General Dynamics, confirmed that getting the UK encryption module into the Harris radio within the program's time frame was viewed as one of the major program risks. They focused the design team on one mission during the bid process: "Do whatever it takes to get the module into the radio and demonstrate it to the customer before the selection decision is made."

They got creative because they didn't have the time to do otherwise.

The team came up with ways to demonstrate the product working with the integrated UK encryption and other key program capabilities. Believing that the competitive team had a significant head start, the Harris engineers had to shorten what would have been a multiyear development down to a three-month time frame. To accomplish this, they tapped into relationships that they had developed with other GD subcontractors and were able to use a UK encryption module that had already been developed by another subcontractor on an earlier program for a similar radio. Harris focused its efforts on developing a clever interface module that allowed the engineers to quickly integrate it into their standard radio product. In the end, the same basic solution was used in final product design.

What can any sales professional learn from this winning effort? If you want to win the sale in a highly competitive situation:

- Provide an early, convincing demonstration that you have the right solution.
- Prepare as carefully to win internal support as you do to win the sale.
- Get the right message to the right decision makers.

The Core of Law 7: Make It a Team Effort

Few great things are accomplished solely by an individual, so gain the commitment of your team and take the lead in making your customer vision a reality.

PART III

WIN

TIPS AND TECHNIQUES FOR GETTING RESULTS, ACCOMPLISHING PRIORITIES, AND CREATING CONTINUING SUCCESS

Law 8: Build Lasting Success
Law 9: Drive Toward Exceptional Results
Law 10: Manage Multiple Customer Priorities

"Surviving is winning, because if you are the last man standing, as they say, then you are the last man standing."
—RICHARD D. PARSONS, CHAIRMAN AND CEO,
AOL TIME WARNER, INC.

Success Magazine asks all of its new employees to share their definition of success. In a feature article about these responses, each new employee, from twentysomething to fiftysomething, offered a unique viewpoint. Victoria Conte, president and publisher, said "At the end of the day, success is knowing that I helped better someone's life."

I believe that professional success should be balanced with personal success. When some people become wealthy or famous, they find that it's not enough. Those who work and live for success should consider whether they'll be happy when they get the success they seek.

To be successful, one must keep in mind the principles that guide one's work and life—without them, it's easy to get sidetracked. If you have these principles clearly in mind and act consistently with them, you will avoid second-guessing your decisions.

In the movie *Citizen Kane*, the main character takes over as publisher of a newspaper. He publishes what he calls a "Declaration of Principles" on the front page of the paper that states that the paper will present the news honestly. If someone were to ask you what the principles are that you or your company operate by, how would you respond?

> *"So every leader, and every employee, needs to be clear about their identity—their values, their beliefs—which provides an anchor in rough waters. Let me conclude by mentioning a few of these anchors, each of them essential for a leader to succeed and for a company to step up to its social responsibility.*
>
> *"The first is integrity, which is non-negotiable. Integrity is the foundation for trust, without which a leader isn't going to lead anybody anywhere. Second is personal accountability—another non-negotiable. Third is a concern for people—treating your employees and public alike with candor and respect. The fourth, and last, is leading by example."*
>
> —Kenneth I. Chenault, chairman and CEO, American
> Express Company, from his keynote address,
> NYU Stern's Graduate Precommencement
> Ceremony, May 14, 2003

BUILD LASTING SUCCESS

There are three principles I suggest as universal in application and of fundamental importance to long-term success: integrity, stability, and purpose.

Integrity

The first quality that a successful sales leader must possess to be successful *in the long term* is integrity. Integrity means doing the right thing, even when doing something less than the right thing would be expedient.

Why is integrity so important? It exemplifies trust. If someone loses trust in you, that trust is difficult to reclaim. There are prominent instances of companies whose salespeople were pushed to fulfill ever-increasing sales quotas to meet ever-increasing Wall Street expectations. Unfortunately, deals were made that sacrificed future profits for present sales and the sales had to keep getting larger to fuel the disappearing profits until, like a pyramid scheme, the financial structure collapsed. At that point, the future survival of what had been a highly valued and respected company was thrown into question.

In one sales workshop I facilitated, the salespeople for a company that was a leader in the health care field were asking how they could compete against salespeople from another company who gave away extravagant gifts to customers. Their company did not permit such excessive gifts. I asked the salespeople to write down what they enjoyed most about their jobs and what they believed in. They cited the following as what they enjoyed most:

- Helping people
- The look on a patient's face after treatment
- Improving human quality of life
- Working with people
- The recognition that comes from working with the number-one company in the field
- Financial rewards

They said they believed that they had the product line that most effectively helps people enjoy their lives again.

These responses mirrored their company's mission. When salespeople are this closely aligned with their company's mission, they know they are making valued contributions, and it allows them to sell consistent with their beliefs.

When speaking with a doctor who might look for expensive gifts, this company's salespeople can set themselves apart by providing a copy of their mission and explaining what they believe in (helping people achieve quality of life, for example). They plant a question in the doctor's mind about a company that feels compelled to use lavish gifts to win customer loyalty rather than the quality of their products.

This company's products and services stand on their own. This is positioning. It means placing your company and yourself in customers' minds as people who believe in what they are doing, believe in the quality and benefits of the products and services they offer, and believe in working with customers in the most ethical manner. The salesperson can even use a statement such as, "If that sounds like the way you like to work, we can work together to help your patients and your practice." If the customer says yes, this is the kind of customer the salesperson would want to work with. If the answer is not an unqualified yes, the salesperson should go on to the next customer. This approach is, in effect, a way of testing whether you have a common set of values with customers and whether they would be a good fit with you and your company.

Avoid any possibility of your integrity being questioned. The consequences of a loss of integrity can be severe, such as loss of business or loss of an account, and it can take an incredible amount of resources to try to recover. It was reported that Enron's board suspended their code of ethics for a short time to allow the company to complete certain financial transactions that otherwise would have been in conflict with their policy. The board's unusual action in and of itself threw suspicion onto other business policies, hampering the company's ability to continue to function normally.

Stability

Most of the sales leaders I've had the opportunity to work with are not the types who act in haste. They tend to find out the facts, look at options, and then act in a considered manner. Their composure leads others to feel a similar level of confidence. They don't overreact. They don't underreact. They tend not to fly off the handle, saying things that they know they would come to regret or that could seriously undermine their credibility with customers.

Different people react differently to the same problem, depending on what they think or feel about it. Most of the sales leaders I've met exemplified the best of all possible attitudes: unafraid of challenges, not put off by circumstances they didn't like, and respectful of their customers. Sales leaders must unhesitatingly demonstrate the attitude they expect from others on their team. They thrive on crises because they are opportunities to model the right attitude.

Sales leaders strive to rise to the occasion. They know that when times are at their worst, they have to be their best. Stability helps them be their best. While they may be composed and in control, they are not without emotions. Those emotions can galvanize them into action and help them persuade others to follow suit.

Their emotions may relate to the work at hand (getting the best quality or meeting a deadline, for example) or the people involved in the situation (being empathetic and supportive, for example). Stability helps a ship stay afloat when buffeted by high winds and seas. Effective leaders call on a similar strength.

"When I have to make an important decision, I've learned to ask myself two questions: 'What is in my best interests?' and 'What is in the best interests of my family?'"

—Stuart Rosenstein, Ph.D.

Frank Digioia is the president of FORT Productions, a multimillion-dollar video production company. His company has grown dramatically. When I asked him what he's learned about success over the decade that he has had his company, he said, "One important thing I've learned about success is that when you think you've arrived and you think it's going to get easier, you're going to work just as hard to maintain it. It's just that the work is different. It might be customer service; it might be team issues."

I also asked him what advice he would give to people who would like to increase their sales by a quantum leap. He said, "They can't expect it to happen overnight. It happens from a series of fundamentals executed over time. I constantly see new salespeople who go into sales and see the money someone made but don't see what the person did to get there. Salespeople need to overcome the 'biorhythms of sales.' The winners plough through the slump. When they are at the top of their game, they are out working with the customers. When they are not at the top of their game, they are getting ready to be."

How to Lead During a Crisis

It is most important to maintain your composure. People are looking to you as the role model. Despite whatever concerns you might have, you need to remain calm. People will use your tone of voice and your body language to assess how composed you are. Give them reasons to be confident.

Communicate with people firsthand, whether that entails group or individual meetings. Candidly answer questions, but don't convey a sense of panic. Instead, work to convey assurance. Assess the situation. Ask others for their assessment and recommendations. Avoid knee-jerk reactions. Be measured in your responses. Work with your team to develop a plan. Look at options and assumptions.

Don't procrastinate making a decision if one is needed. Move ahead and then, if necessary, revise your strategy as more information becomes known. Decide whether the situation calls for a unilateral decision on your part or for a consensus approach. You may need to move between both types of decisions—for example, by unilaterally deciding to ask a team to use a consensus approach in arriving at a decision.

Be empathetic. If you don't feel the same concern that others do, at least try to understand in your own way what they are feeling and let them know that their feelings are valid. It's human to have emotions, and you can show them in an appropriate way.

Purpose

How are you successful as a sales leader? You probably care a great deal about what you do and why you do it. Sure, you probably like to make money. But if you could make all the money you could ever want but felt unfulfilled and bored, how long do you think it would be before you would decide to do something else that made you feel challenged and significant? Exceptional sales leaders have a personal *mission* and a purpose for what they do that rises above the ordinary. Their goals are aligned with that mission.

A purpose is a constant in the midst of ever-changing objectives. If you remain focused on it, you will achieve meaningful objectives. Purpose is like an engine, providing power and propulsion. Goals and objectives provide direction and a destination. We need both.

What do you care about? To what lengths would you go to demonstrate it? Are you doing what you care about?

It is hard to imagine anything great being accomplished without someone caring a great deal about accomplishing it. The depth of your devotion to a goal or purpose will determine how energetically you tackle problems. It will determine your enthusiasm and that of others you want to influence to join you in your effort. It will determine your ability to persevere when you face setbacks.

For example, when you care about something, you won't easily settle for no as an answer, whether that is winning a tough sale or leading a challenging project. You become creative, looking for solutions instead of looking for excuses. You get others excited. You accomplish the impossible. Think about what you care about. What have you always enjoyed doing? What do you dream about? What gets you excited? If you don't know, make it your goal to find out. Read, talk to others, follow your curiosity, and trust your instincts.

Did He Have Passion?

In a popular movie, one of the lead actors says toward the end, "The Greeks didn't write obituaries. They just asked, 'Did he have passion?'" That struck me as meaningful, regardless of whether the Greeks actually wrote obituaries or not. Living without passion is like living without life. There isn't much excitement, there isn't much sparkle, and there isn't much to look forward to. So why wouldn't it be a good idea to assess the sum of our lives by assessing how much passion we had about what we did, who we were, or what we lived for? From time to time I see newspaper stories about people who were outstanding in their lives, people who did things that made them memorable. Their acts might have set records or simply have modeled unselfishness. In each case, there is usually an element of greatness about how they lived and who they were.

Movies entertain, but they often communicate a message. I especially like the ones that are based on true stories or are inspirational, and I've seen some that are particularly applicable for people who want to be sales leaders. The movie *Music of the Heart* offers a good example of what a difference passion can make. It is based on the true story of a woman whose passion for music helped her to achieve not only her immediate goal of landing a job, but to inspire students to find greatness in themselves and parents to creatively work together to save a school music program. Another is *Mr. Holland's Opus*. One more movie to see is *Rudy,* based on a true story about a boy who dreams of going to Notre Dame and playing on their football team, which seems like an impossible dream because everyone says he is too small to play. These movies inspire because they're about people who accomplished a great deal because they cared a great deal.

> *"If I were to see myself the way you see me, I would have to retire."*
> —Steven Spielberg

The Core of Law 8: Build Lasting Success

Sustain your success by always acting with integrity, maintaining stability, and acting consistently with the values that best serve your company and your customers.

DRIVE TOWARD EXCEPTIONAL RESULTS

Several key elements will contribute to your success. The first is the solutions you deliver to customers. A second element is your boss. A third is how effectively you influence people with your proposals. And a fourth is how well you communicate your ideas in your presentations. This section will cover the last three areas.

Managing Up

It's not unusual for someone to remark to me, "The challenge I have isn't with the people I work with—it's with the person I work for. How do I manage up?" Everyone who rises to a leadership position in an organization has worked for someone who is difficult to work for.

Sometimes the person is difficult to work for because he or she was promoted into the job based on sales or technical skills rather than on solid people skills. Sometimes the person may just have a different style. Sometimes the person may not realize there is a better way to manage. Here are seven solutions for those situations.

- Remember that the situation won't last forever. At some point, something will change. The boss will get promoted, the boss will leave, you may move to a new job. Knowing this gives you the ability to take one day at a time.

- Ask yourself what you can learn from this person. Your boss may have skills or strengths that you can learn from—try to look for them. If nothing else, you can at least learn what *not* to do. This can be highly valuable.
- As long as the person doesn't ask you to do anything illegal or unethical, try to put yourself in his or her shoes. Try to understand what he or she really wants. Then, despite whatever misgivings you may have about whether it is the correct decision, put your best effort behind it. If you give it only a halfhearted effort or none at all, that will be obvious and limiting. Rather than head for that type of confrontation, work proactively to manage the situation.
- If your boss puts off making decisions that you need in order to do your job, provide him or her with a recommended course of action based on your analysis of several possible options. The way you present your recommendation is important. Don't present it as asking for a decision. Suggest that you have identified the best way to proceed. Even if your boss disagrees with your choice and advises another path, at least you have a decision and can move ahead. It is a better approach than waiting for a decision that may not come.
- If your boss gives you something to do but then never follows up, schedule a follow-up meeting *at the time* you are given the assignment. Make clear ahead of time that the purpose of the followup meeting is to make whatever decisions are required in order to move ahead. Proceed as described in the fourth item in this list.
- If you are having a difficult time getting priorities from your boss, or you are expected to do everything or add tasks to the top of your pile without regard to what you are already working on, develop a set of priorities to present to your boss for his or her concurrence. Set priorities based on your estimate of the value the task will contribute to your organization. Use a simple numbering scheme, such as using 1 to designate the most important task, 2 for the next most important task, and so on. Show these to your boss

and ask him or her to evaluate and revise them as necessary, making it clear that you will proceed based on these priorities. You may also want to show deadlines and resource estimates.

- If your estimate shows you don't have enough time by yourself to complete all your assignments and you know your boss wants them all done, develop a plan for accomplishing them. See if you can get overtime authorized. Borrow people, bring in contract personnel or interns, develop a technology solution, or find other creative solutions.

"To be confident, fake it initially, and then scramble to come up with the goods. Confidence is something for me that I struggled with and still struggle with."

—Julia Roberts, actor

Managing Projects

Sales professionals will be called on to manage or participate in projects. They often win large sales that require support from multiple departments and extensive coordination with the customer's organization in order to implement. I won't try to re-create a project management course here, but I would like to share some of the best practices I've learned from managing many large projects and from my research.

Although projects involve a set of schedules, costs, and requirements, when it comes down to it they are primarily about people—getting them to commit to the goals of the project and to work together to bring it to a successful conclusion. Most of the problems that people run into on projects revolve around issues of communication (clear goals, for example) and commitment (having allegiance to their department or their own projects). Granted, there are excellent project management techniques that can be used to expedite the project and keep it on course. But the best project management tools will not compensate for poor support, misalignment, or resistance. On the other hand, with the right people and the right commitment, they will find ways to get around any obstacle. You have probably seen instances of that level of commitment in your own work experience.

One of the most common reasons that projects fail is that they have unclear goals. People think they know what they are supposed to be doing and what they are trying to accomplish, but it often isn't the case. The goal needs to be specific and measurable, quantitatively and qualitatively. Projects also languish when they don't have the high level of support they need. In some cases, projects never come to fruition because of multiple problems.

Winning Proposals

When you work hard to win the right to make a bid on a large sale, you don't want to lose the sale because of the way your proposal is presented. Consider the following important tips.

- *Your proposal must look professional.* How you achieve that professional look depends on the size of the sale, the expectations of the person receiving it, and the technology you have to use. Be sure your facts are straight. Provide backup or references for statistics or conclusions you reach in your proposal. Have a colleague or even a team double-check your final draft.
- *Be sure there are no typos.* Some people reject anything when they find a typo, however arbitrary that may seem. Get someone who is a great proofreader to read over your proposal. A good but time-consuming way to pick up typos is to have someone read it backward. That ensures that someone will not skip over a word that is misspelled by reading too quickly.
- *Organize the proposal in a way that is easy to follow.* Include an executive overview that is no longer than one page. The overview should describe the major benefits of your proposal in terms of financial benefit and positive effect on the customer's organization and customers. It should also highlight how the proposal addresses the concerns and problems of the customer that you and members of the

customer's team uncovered and a recommendation for the next step. Give an overview of what is in the rest of the proposal and why it is there.

- *Make your proposal easy to read.* Readers should not have to struggle to understand jargon, bad grammar, or long run-on sentences. Avoid frequent use of the passive voice; it is confusing and weak. (For example, "The decision was made" is stated in the passive voice. "The project team decided" is stated in the active voice.) The active voice leads people to think that you believe in what you are saying.

- *If you can use graphics to illustrate a point, do so.* A picture is quickly understood. Don't let glitz detract from the content. Don't overwhelm what you have to say with too much color, too many fonts, or unusual designs. Less is more.

- *Find ways to get your customer actively involved in reviewing the proposal.* You could have a set of questions that you display and will answer as you go through the proposal. You can have a discussion and answer questions as you complete each part. You don't want to be the only one talking and you don't want to wait until you have finished to get customer feedback.

- *Address the concerns of others who may be reviewing the proposal.* If you are presenting a proposal to your contact, who will then present it to a committee that you will not be able to attend, ask the customer if he or she is personally convinced your proposal is the right approach. Make sure you have addressed the concerns of the decision influencers as well as the decision makers.

Presentation Skills

When you are going before customers, executives, or team members, how you present can be almost as important as what you say. Some executives speaking to groups come across as unfocused when they are supposed to be inspiring. They may be capable leaders in other respects, but their stature is diminished when they present their ideas. There are many executives who do inspire people with their presentations. They do it in their own style, but they come across as sincere, thoughtful, and prepared. Here are several tips for getting ready to do a presentation.

Prepare

The more important the presentation, the more you want to overprepare. When you are prepared, you will be confident. You will know the key points you want to make, why you want to make them, and how you will make them. You will be prepared for contingencies, such as when you need to trim some time from your presentation. You will be better equipped to answer tough questions, rather than hesitating to find suitable answers. You will be better able to anticipate and address concerns that the audience will have.

Gil Eagles, CSP, CPAE, a professional speaker, once told me that there are two questions you must answer to do an effective presentation: What do you have to say, and why should your audience listen? As a presenter, you need to be clear about the message you want to leave with your audience and convey it in a way that makes it memorable. Gil also said that audiences typically want one of two things: to be educated or to be entertained. If they expect to learn something new, they won't be happy just being entertained. Giving them both—information and inspiration—will encourage them to listen and act on your advice.

Know your audience. This is critical. Find out who is going to be in the audience. What is their present level of knowledge? What are their interests and concerns? Who are the experts and the influencers? How do they like to receive information (bottom-line, quick, to the point; or more detailed, thorough, and precise)? Find out about the current issues and trends affecting their business and their industry. Be ready to address a significant recent or pending event.

To touch your audience at an emotional level, provide not only facts and data but examples or stories that illustrate the points you are making. People remember stories and the principles they illustrate long after they forget the facts.

Let me offer a couple of thoughts on using computer visuals. Many people have seen so many computer presentations that they have lost their impact. Often these visuals don't even add much to the presentation, and in fact may detract from it. However, because some customers prefer that you present information using the computer, you should know how to make them effective. The following guidelines will help.

- Keep the visual information to a minimum. The first error that many presenters make is to load up the visual with a lot of information. This applies for both written and graphic information.
- Don't just read what's on the overhead. If you're just going to read it, why does the audience need you? Instead, comment on the importance, relevance, applicability, or other factors concerning the points you have on the visual. Tie the points together.
- I tend not to use visuals that contain nothing more than a list of points that are already in a handout. I might make an exception if I don't have a handout and I would like to use the visual as a reminder of what I want to say, or to give the people in the audience who have a preference for receiving information visually something to look at. Use visuals that add color or graphics, or that can be built up as part of a slide show.
- If you eliminate some visuals, it gives the others greater impact. It is also easier to keep track of them, and you won't need to spend much time looking at notes about them. You will also have less of a tendency to sound as if you are reading. Have a printout of the visuals you are using.
- Personalize the visuals for your audience. If you are giving a proposal or recommendation to a customer, use their logo (get it from their Web site or have them E-mail you a copy), speak their language, and address their issues.

Some people debate whether you should distribute handouts before or after your presentation. My recommendation is generally to give the handout ahead of your presentation, rather than afterward, with this caveat: if you're concerned that people might be looking ahead in the handout while you are on a page, ask them not to. I sometimes ask people to raise their hand and repeat after me: "I do solemnly pledge not to move ahead in the handout until instructed to do so." Most people chuckle about this, and they even sometimes join in by reminding me later when I ask them to look ahead to another page. I sometimes joke that I will pay careful attention to those people whose lips were moving but weren't saying anything.

Practice

At one time, I felt that practicing my presentation might take away the spontaneity. It doesn't. When you practice, you become more comfortable with what you are going to say. This allows you to concentrate on the audience and their responses when you are doing your presentation, rather than concentrating on what you are going to say next.

Practicing doesn't mean memorizing. You may want to memorize your opening and closing words, but even when you do that, you don't want to sound as if you are reading from a prepared text. You want it to sound natural. You don't need to memorize each point. If you have a handout or electronic presentation, that will give you an easy way to remember key points. Your detailed knowledge of the subject and your preparation will allow you to fill in the details. Practice how you emphasize the important words, your tone of voice, and your body language. Don't exaggerate or be melodramatic, but don't be boring.

There are several ways to practice. You can practice by yourself. If you do, it's a good idea to record yourself using either audio or video. That way you will know how you come across. You can practice in front of others in order to gauge their reactions and get their suggestions. For a critical presentation, practice at least three times.

Present

When you get to the presentation, you will be prepared. Arrive early, make sure everything is set up as you requested, and be prepared to make changes if it isn't. Greet people and speak with people who will be in the audience—people you know or, even better, people you don't know—to build rapport, gain a couple of new friends and allies, and do some last-minute research or validation of your examples or points.

When you begin your presentation, begin by taking a breath and pausing. Don't rush. You want to be in control and give that appearance to your audience. Begin your presentation with a compelling fact, a startling observation, or a question—something that grabs the audience's attention right away. Then quickly give the audience useful information. Get to the heart of the matter right away. What I have found is that early impressions shape the perception of the remainder of the presentation. You want people to know that what you are presenting is valuable and will be worth their time. Use your time judiciously.

Look at the individuals in the audience. Make eye contact with someone for a complete thought or a complete sentence. This is one of the things you should practice. Most of us are comfortable speaking with people one on one. To be more comfortable and in control when you are in front of an audience, regardless of how big that audience is, just think of it as speaking with people one on one. If you make eye contact with an individual, people in the audience will feel as if you are speaking directly to them. Be sure not to overlook people. The person you overlook may feel insulted and later, when you are looking for support, may undermine that support. This person may be a decision influencer.

If you are a little nervous when you begin your presentation, that nervousness will soon subside if you have prepared and practiced. A bit of anxiety is normal. It gets your adrenaline flowing and gives you energy. That's why it is so important to practice, especially the beginning of your presentation. Be yourself. Don't try to be someone else.

Be sure to make your presentation interactive. You can do this by asking questions, asking for examples, or even asking people to raise their hands in response to a question about how many of them have ever experienced a certain phenomenon (such as saving a little on a purchase but ultimately spending a lot more). When you prepare, consider how to keep the audience engaged.

Be sure to have a strong closing. Take questions before you finish, and then end with a quick story or summary.

People Skills

People in sales jobs tend to have strong sales skills and product knowledge. Those skills are essential for success in a sales job, but good people skills are just as important. The more you want to influence people, the more you need a good balance between sales and people skills.

When I was promoted into my first management job, it was because I had demonstrated good technical and organizational skills. My people skills weren't a problem, but I didn't need them as much as I did when I moved into management. As a manager, much of my job involved getting work done through my staff.

All was well until we had an extra-heavy workload and my people skills were tested. I had worked diligently to get better at working with people and was fortunate that I had the opportunity to do so after realizing that I needed to. Everyone has blind spots.

A lack of good people skills is one of the most common reasons that people on the fast track get derailed on their way to the top or dethroned once they get there. The farther up you are in an organization, the more you need people skills to be successful. It makes sense. You must work through people to get things done. You can't do it all yourself.

The basics of good people skills might seem self-evident, but let's take a moment to consider one of the most important people skills: tact. Tact is being able to get your point across diplomatically. It means broaching a sensitive subject in a way that keeps the other person listening and engaged. It may mean using conditional terms, such as "Perhaps you should consider this." Using tact allows the other person to maintain his or her self-esteem. It actually gives you greater control in most cases than being direct. There are times when you need to be direct and not conditional. But it pays to save that approach for the rare times that it is needed rather than rely on it as a daily way of interacting with people. If it is reserved for the times when it is really needed, it will create the desired effect of getting people to do what you want without alienating them, as long as you take a moment to explain why you are asking the person to do what you are asking.

People with leadership responsibilities sometimes come to rely too much on their authority in order to accomplish their goals. They believe that they are required to make the decisions and give orders because they have been given those leadership responsibilities, but that isn't the case. They simply need to get certain things done, and there are a variety of ways to do it.

Sometimes you see strong salespeople who steamroll over those who get in their way. They may even do this with the customer, when, for example, they go over the customer's head to try to make the sale. Sometimes they are successful in the short term, but because of the extensive damage they do to relationships, their power usually catches up with them down the road when someone undermines them. Sales leaders use good people skills coupled with their sales skills to get the best of both worlds.

> *"Nobody is going to give anything to us. We have to earn their business each and every day, in everything we do."*
>
> —Pat Russo, CEO, Lucent Technologies

The Core of Law 9: Drive Toward Exceptional Results

Develop your people, proposal, and presentation skills so that they are as good as your technical and sales skills.

MANAGE MULTIPLE CUSTOMER PRIORITIES

What are your biggest time wasters?

Interruptions
Management by crisis
Lack of priorities
Conflicting goals
Meetings
Disorganization
Procrastination
Voice mail
E-mail

How many of these apply to you? Did you find that you don't have any time wasters of significance? Or did you, like most people, recognize at least a couple that cut into your productivity? All of the items on the list except "Lack of priorities" and "Conflicting goals" are activities that we can control to some degree—and even those two items are activities we can handle proactively.

Most sales professionals have a discretionary control over their time. But if you find that you occasionally spend time on activities that are not highly productive, it is worthwhile to change how you handle them. If you don't use your time as productively as you should due to outside influences or your own distractions, take corrective action. It is impossible to be a sales leader with unproductive work habits or interferences.

The most common time waster is interruptions. That's true whether those interruptions come from a cell phone, a pager, a phone, or a visitor. I find that many salespeople have a high interest in finding ways to use their time more effectively.

How to Control Interruptions

How much time do you lose each day to interruptions? Thirty minutes? An hour? Two hours? Are most or these interruptions of value? When you are interrupted, do you find that when you go back to what you were working on it takes almost as long to get back to where you were as it took to do the work originally? If so, all the work you did originally and all the time you invested are wasted. If you are one of the many people who are constantly interrupted, you'll benefit enormously when you use the ideas that follow to better control interruptions. It helps to know that there are three types of interruptions:

- The personal interruption
- The wrong-time interruption
- The good interruption

Knowing the difference between these three and what to do about them will help you control them. You won't eliminate interruptions, but you can control them more effectively.

The *personal interruption* occurs when someone wants to chat—about the weekend, the game, the party, or whatever. The quick solution is to say that you have a deadline for a proposal, or other work you must finish, and that you'll catch up with the visitor another time. If you are managing your time well, you really will have a deadline and something to complete, so you are just being honest.

The *wrong-time interruption* happens when you want to speak to the person interrupting you, but at a later time. Use a similar response to the personal interruption, but more structured. First, if you are in the middle of writing or reading, keep your work posture. Look up with your eyes, but don't raise your head. (It sends the first signal that you are reluctant to be interrupted.) Don't put your pen or pencil down. Don't sit back in your chair. Instead, let the person know you are aware of him or her but that you have a deadline to meet, and then propose to visit when you're done or at the earliest time possible for you.

Most people will accept this alternative. Some will insist that they must see you now. Sometimes they may even get annoyed that you won't see them now. The best way to handle these situations is to alert people you normally work with before the next interruption. Explain ahead of time that there are certain times you prefer not to be interrupted. Explain why, and whenever possible, show them how it benefits them. People resist change; this gives them a chance to adjust.

A woman at one of my seminars worked for seven bosses. She told them, "When I have my pink cap on, it's not a good time to interrupt me." The pink cap may not be for you, but how about a traffic cone? That's what one manager told me she did. When I replied that it was a novel idea and asked where she got the cone, she said she'd rather not discuss it. If you communicate to people why you're doing something and do it with humor, people are more willing to accept it.

The *good interruption* happens when you must speak with the person now. It could be because it affects what you're working on now or because it affects another high-value activity that must be handled urgently (in other words, a crisis).

If you agree to stop what you are doing, get your papers and thoughts organized so that when you go back to them you can quickly recapture your thoughts. You should also set up a time frame: how long would it take to resolve this issue? Don't leave it open-ended. Get agreement to the time needed and explain that this way you'll be able to get back to your deadline. Stick to the time frame. Thank the person for his or her cooperation.

Most interruptions are of the untimely type. Unfortunately, too often we treat them as if they are appropriate. If someone approached you and asked for ten dollars, would you give it up? In most cases, probably not. Why, then, are we so willing to give ten minutes of our time? Don't give up on controlling interruptions. Even if you haven't been able to control them before, you will with the methods I've outlined here, and the payoff will be that you'll be able to concentrate your efforts and get your work done more quickly with better results.

Set aside blocks of time (thirty to sixty minutes) to complete work where you need to work uninterrupted. Let your calls go to voice mail or have someone else handle them during that time. Again, it's impossible to eliminate interruptions—but you can and should control them.

After a discussion during a program about how to control interruptions, one of the participants remarked to me that her customers were her interruptions. She worked in a bank and could not ignore the customers, she said. She added that she was required to submit a report every week and couldn't find the hour it took to complete it during normal business hours. I recommended that she ask a knowledgeable colleague to help the customers during the hour that it takes her to complete the report and that she try to arrange this during a slow time for the bank (not on Monday or Friday, for example). That is what I mean by *controlling* interruptions. (A bonus: she could also use the opportunity to delegate responsible tasks to someone she saw as having the potential to take on more responsibility.)

Think Time

A fellow who came up with a radically new design for a computer chip gained the insight about how to do it while he was walking during an extended time away from work. It was one of those eureka moments, he said. He said that he realized after thinking about the problem for some time that the difficulty with the current design methods for computer chips was that the instructions were wired into the chip. The chips got bigger and hotter as a result. He realized that many of the functions of the chip could be handled by software, which would lower the energy requirements. This is especially important for notebook computers. His design is in use in some notebook computers as a result of the insight he gained that day. If he had not given his mind a quiet time, he never would have realized the answer to the problem he had been working on for some time.

Give yourself time to plan and think. If you are going to be a leader in your field and make breakthroughs, you need to think about problems creatively. This is critical to your ability to come up with innovative solutions. It may even be a way to see problems differently and challenge the status quo as a result.

> *"If you're an artist and you've had some success, you should pull back at some point and go back to square one. The only thing that endures is change."*
>
> —Robert Redford, actor

Time Wasters and Time Challenges

Eliminate or delegate time wasters; control time challenges. Time wasters are activities such as putting together sales kits, reporting information, and nonessential E-mail. Time challenges are activities such as preparing proposals, precall planning, and learning new products. A time waster is an activity that doesn't add value to what you do for your customers. It makes you less effective. A time challenge is an activity you need to do for your job, but could do more efficiently.

Cut Meeting Time in Half

Almost everyone agrees that too much time is wasted in meetings. It doesn't have to be that way; that time can easily be cut in half.

In a program I did with a longtime client, the AAA East Penn, we discussed the principles of running more effective meetings, which they called a *code of meeting ethics*. I like the name as a way of emphasizing the respect that people need to give each other in order to have meetings that work well. The list includes seven items and is shown on the next page. Some groups have principles such as these posted in any meeting they hold as a way of reminding people of how they have agreed to conduct their meetings.

As a sales professional, if you are running the meeting, take advantage of the code of meeting ethics. If you are a meeting participant, suggest to the meeting facilitator that you persuade the group to agree to follow this code. Put it on display. People who have adopted just the time-allotted agenda and the timekeeper ideas are enthusiastic about the results in time saved.

All the items listed will work for audio or video teleconferences as well as face-to-face meetings. Be sure to cover these principles at the beginning of the meeting and get concurrence from people to adhere to them. If you find that your meetings still last too long or aren't as focused as you would like, don't discard these suggestions. Give them time. It may take three or four meetings before people get comfortable working within the new parameters.

People who have used this approach have told me that their meetings are shorter and more productive. They say no one would ever want to return to the unproductive meetings they had before. I believe you can cut your meeting time in half and get more done when you follow these practices.

Code of Meeting Ethics
- Have a clear purpose or objective for the meeting. (For example, to gather customer data or to present a customer proposal.) Otherwise, don't hold it.
- Start on time and end on time.
- Make the meeting shorter rather than longer. If anything, end a few minutes early.
- Have an agenda. Send it out before the meeting. Stick to it.
  - Use a *time-allotted agenda* (a start and stop time for each *item* on the agenda).
  - Have a *timekeeper* (someone who keeps the meeting on time).
  - Have a *gatekeeper* (someone who keeps everyone participating).
- Be respectful of others' points of view. Avoid sidebar conversations. One person talks at a time.

- Summarize decisions, people responsible for follow-up, and due dates. Develop an action plan; set the next meeting dates in advance.
- Ask people to turn off cell phones while in the meeting. Minimize interruptions.

Get Organized

I haven't observed many disorganized salespeople. Even if you aren't a person who is normally highly organized, if you are successful in sales it's because you have worked to compensate for any inclination to be disorganized. But if you are looking for ways to become more organized, you might find the following discussion helpful.

Disorganization actually starts as a state of mind. Disorganized people tend to be comfortable with disorganization, seeing it as inevitable. They may even wear it as a badge of honor. Unfortunately, others may perceive them as being ineffective, even if they aren't.

How does disorganization become evident? First and foremost is the desk, work area, cubicle, home office, or car. These are the most visible to you and offer stark feedback about how organized (or disorganized) you are. I've found that it usually takes a lot less time to clean up an area than I think it will. And once I do clean it up, I find that I feel much more organized. When you look at your desk or work area and it looks disorganized, you subconsciously think, "If I can't control my own desk, what can I control?" When you feel you don't have control, your stress level goes up. So one of the best ways to lower stress and be more productive is to clean up your work area.

The quickest way to clean up the work area is to get some boxes and take what's on top of the desk and place it in the boxes. Label the boxes "desktop as of [date]." By doing this, you'll know where everything is, but things won't distract you on your desk. You can leave on the desk anything that is an active work project. The best thing is to put those items into vertical trays, not horizontal stacks. If your car is stacked with papers, do the same thing. The key is to ask when was the last time you used the papers, and pack them in the box if you can't remember. The rule is that it always takes longer to find something than it takes to file it.

The second way that salespeople sometimes get disorganized is not planning for appointments. This is one of the three most common mistakes that salespeople make (see page 52). Fortunately, this is correctable with some good planning strategies.

Home Office Challenges

Working at home has its benefits and its challenges. If you are besieged at the office, it may provide relief from the constant stream of interruptions you are likely to encounter there. But working at home can have its challenges as well. Salespeople often have a home office, besides their car.

One of those challenges may be interruptions from people who are at home with you. They may think that because you are "at home" you are available to run errands, handle chores, or help out. You may give in to these distractions yourself. One of the benefits of being at home is that you have some flexibility to handle emergencies and to build your schedule to accommodate personal needs. But without limitations on those demands, you can fall victim to home distractions and your productivity can suffer.

On the other hand, sometimes we need extra patience when we deal with family interruptions. I heard a story about a fellow speaker who became impatient when his child interrupted him because he was in the middle of work. But then he stopped and thought about it and realized he hadn't set a good example. Fortunately, he was able to remedy the situation.

These tips will help you minimize distractions when working at home.

- Let people know that they should not think of you as being in your home office, but in the company's office. How often would they call you or come to see you there? Ask them to respect your work environment at home just as they would if you were at your company office.

- Set up a form of communication to let people know when you are not available. A closed door might be one way to do this. Get a roll of caution tape or a traffic cone at a hardware store and let people know that when the door is closed and the caution tape is up or the traffic cone is out, it is not a good time to interrupt you. Keep the tape or cone up for only a portion of the day.
- Provide limited, structured time when you can be available for giving attention to your family, others, or personal tasks. Let them know what these limits are and why it is important for your family to help you keep them. Do work that requires concentration at times when you are not as likely to be interrupted, such as early morning, school time, or later in the evening. Make phone calls when you know you will have privacy, but don't be overly concerned about the person on the other end of the phone knowing that you work at home. It is becoming commonplace and acceptable to work at home.

Working from a Distance

You may work with remotely located people who are supporting you on a customer solution. Working with people at a distance presents its own unique set of challenges.

The advent of E-mail, instant messaging, cell phones, and audio and video teleconferencing have given us more efficient means of managing at a distance when compared to the more limited means that still may be useful—namely, travel in person, the phone, fax, or letters. We have a variety of ways to communicate quickly with people regardless of where they are. But these communication channels don't change the basic need for good, timely, and purposeful communication.

Distance magnifies differences between people so that dealing even with small problems can become difficult. Here are ten suggestions for working effectively from a distance.

- Be extra clear and specific in your communications.
- Plan what you will say so you don't omit anything.
- Think carefully about *how* you will communicate.

- Give the people you are communicating with time to plan.
- Build in time for periodic face-to-face meetings.
- Rotate meetings with people in different locations.
- Use weekly audio teleconference calls to keep people up to date on changes in products or services or for training.
- Use daily audio calls for people having difficulties.
- Think in terms of results, not just activities.
- Use technology to its full advantage, including E-learning.

Language Differences Matter

There are many diverse cultures in the workforce and in customer organizations. When you encounter people whose native language is not the same as yours, slow down, be patient, repeat what you hear, and use illustrations when possible. I've found that I can usually start to understand most accents, given enough time to pick up the cadence. If you find it difficult to listen to someone's voice, concentrate instead on listening for the content of what the person is saying. Write down key points as a way to concentrate on what the person is saying rather than how he or she is saying it.

SEVEN PERSONAL PLANNING TIPS

- Always ask yourself, *Is what I am working on right now the best use of my time?* How will you know if it is the best use of your time? It will be the best use if:
    - It is going to help you achieve your goals
    - It is the item with the highest value to you, your customers, or your company
    - It can't be delegated
- Rather than focusing on when you need to finish something, focus on when you need to start. Then start when you need to. One reason projects and tasks don't get finished on time is that we think we have plenty of time, so we put off the important work in favor of the urgent items—until the important becomes urgent.

- Schedule the most important work during the time when your energy is highest. The earlier in the day, the better. Take control of the day before it takes control of you. Don't put off doing things you don't like doing but are necessary.
- Plan what you will work on. If you don't have a plan you will tend to allow yourself to be interrupted, distracted, and delayed from accomplishing what is most important to you. You would usually not consider taking a vacation without planning it out. Why does your work deserve any less?
- Recognize that you will need to make adjustments. There will always be some interruptions. There will be changes in the work that must be done. Build into your schedule some time for interruptions and new or unexpected work. When you have a "margin of safety" it helps you maintain control.
- Whenever you have a choice, don't cram things together. If one of the activities runs late, you'll be rushing from one project to the next or one appointment to the next. That creates additional stress that you don't need. Allow some extra minutes between appointments, for example, so that you won't be as rushed.
- Keep your desk or work area free of clutter. Clutter distracts you from your primary task. It also creates additional stress. Keeping things in order promotes a feeling of control.

Principles of Proactive Planning
- Planning takes time; not planning takes more time.
- It takes a lot less to prevent a crisis than it takes to solve it.
- You can't eliminate interruptions, but you can control them.

Review your results for the day with these questions:

- Did you accomplish your most important priority?
- What trends do you notice about how you spent your time?
- What was the most productive part of your day? Why?
- What was the least productive part of your day? Why?
- What or who caused the majority of interruptions?
- What could you do to control these interruptions?
- What was your biggest time waster?

portant priority is deciding what my priorities are."
—Anonymous sales executive

ₛs are bound to come from time to time. When a crisis happens,
ₛse control of the situation. As we manage through the crisis, we
ₑmpt to regain control. (Some of us are crisis managers. We say, "I
ₗo my best work under pressure.") The only way to prevent the same
type of crisis from happening again is to learn from it, to debrief after
the crisis is over, to understand the root causes behind the crisis, and to
take steps to keep them from recurring.

Crisis managers don't have time to do that because as soon as one
crisis has ended, they are moving to the next. Why? It's exciting. They
know what they need to do, and they and everyone else who has to pitch
in to solve the crisis can actually see the objective achieved when the
crisis is over. In the meantime, there is a high cost in terms of resources
and burnout if this continues for too long. Other higher-value work
doesn't get done, which, of course, leads to the next crisis. And so on.

Crisis Contributors

Why do we too often become willing crisis contributors, people who
seem to prefer to work in a crisis environment?

- A crisis can get us energized.
- A crisis pulls people together.
- A crisis gives us a clear goal.
- A crisis requires immediate attention.
- People won't bother us for lower priority work when they know
  we are fighting the "crisis."

Author and consultant Peter Drucker notes that effective people
focus on results, not just activities. Effective people set and stay with
priorities.

Of course, as a sales leader you want to experience as few crises as possible. You must proactively plan ahead and tend to high-value, customer-driven activities.

Five Lessons on Managing Through a Distraction*
- Have a strategic vision and peripheral vision: look ahead, look around.
- Build a strong team. Success is always derived from the right people and teamwork
- Communicate constantly with people through meetings, E-mails, voice mail, and Webcasts.
- Know more about your business than observers or critics do.
- Have a strong internal compass. Know what you need to do, but be flexible.

Crisis Replacers

A crisis gives us excitement, focus, and satisfaction when it's solved. But if we want to get out of the crisis mentality mode we need to find something else that does the same thing. You can't be a crisis manager and sales leader at the same time.

What else can give us excitement, focus, and satisfaction? Achieving worthwhile, challenging goals. Seeing your solutions implemented by your customers will. By actively deciding what we want to achieve and what we want to strive for, we create positive energy and excitement.

The difference between a crisis and a goal is the difference between reacting to the past and problems and focusing on the future and opportunities.

Working in a Crisis-Prone Organization

If you find yourself working in an organization that tends to function at the crisis level, what should you do? First, make sure you have your

---

* Carly Fiorina, CEO, Hewlett-Packard, as reported in the *Wall Street Journal*

own priorities in line. Second, don't be lulled into a crisis mentality. That happens when you get caught up in the activity trap and aren't clear about the difference between activities that add value versus those that don't. Third, maintain your sense of control over your work, but don't promote the perception that you aren't "busy." People who function with a crisis mentality expect others to support the resolution of the crisis. Move quickly, act supportively, and keep an eye on your longer-term, high-value priorities.

Everything Works As a System

We need to think about the system as we define problems and solutions. If we fail to take into account how one change will affect something else, the change will not work or may be ineffective. The change may even backfire.

For example, if you attempt to lower costs, what happens to quality? If you attempt to speed up delivery time, what happens to cost? When you change something in one department, does it affect other people or departments?

There are very few situations in which making one change doesn't affect something else. If these other effects are secondary and you are aware of them, you can either accommodate them or ignore them, as long as you consciously decide.

The Core of Law 10: Manage Customer Priorities

Work efficiently at home, in the office, or remotely with others and use effective planning to avoid or solve a crisis.

CLOSING THOUGHTS
ALWAYS STRIVE TO IMPROVE

We must make a conscious choice to grow in ability and wisdom. Making a conscious decision to grow means taking advantage of every opportunity we are given to learn more about ourselves and the changing world. Making such a choice is a must for a leader, someone who is seen as a model for influencing others to be open to new directions, and someone who wants to continue to be effective at influencing others.

Challenges

Everyone has problems. They may not have them to the same degree or at the same time, but everyone certainly does have them. It can be easy to think that we have problems and others don't. Of course, we don't see what goes on behind the scenes. At a holiday get-together, I glanced around at the people there; some I knew and some I had just met. Some of the people I knew were facing personal challenges. And I knew I had faced my own as well. It made me realize that I was seeing only what people were willing to let others see.

I have a client I first worked with when she was a human resources manager at a manufacturer of color pigments. Her name is Gloria Dittman, and she is currently president of the Edison Chamber of Commerce. She has a philosophy about life that I often quote. She believes, "Whatever happens, happens for the best, provided you find a way to learn or grow from it. You may not see at the time how to do it, but that is how life presents its lessons."

It's up to us to find a way to make the best of situations that we can't rationalize or understand. Adversity can build character. Gloria says, "It makes life easier if you find a way to turn adversity to your advantage."

Mistakes

Everyone makes mistakes—the trick is to avoid making the same ones repeatedly. Learn from yours, and from others' mistakes as well. Make "original" mistakes if you are going to make any. When others make mistakes, your reaction will factor into whether they will take another risk when they do something for you. Most of us know when we have made a mistake. We like to be supported when it happens. We don't like to have it pointed out. If it is pointed out, how it is pointed out becomes critical.

> *"The key thing is, if you make a mistake, have the courage to fix it quickly. I do think the price of inaction is far higher than the cost of making a mistake."*
> —Meg Whitman, CEO, eBay

Perfectionism

There's a big difference between perfectionism and striving for perfection. Striving for perfection means continuing to eliminate the little problems that keep a process, product, or service from surpassing the expectations of the customer. Perfectionism is compulsively trying to do something perfectly, even *when it doesn't matter*. Perfectionists drive themselves and others crazy. They waste time.

Humor

Humor relaxes people. It helps people relate. If you have a gift for using it in the right way, that's great. If not, it's something you can develop. Humor isn't about jokes; it is about looking at the absurdity in a situation. In tense situations, when someone comments on the obvious, people relax and move past the sticking point.

Procrastination

When people don't reach their goals, procrastination is often the culprit. It robs energy, wastes time, and increases stress. Sometimes people procrastinate because they'd rather be doing something more enjoyable. Sometimes it's because they think they are not going to like what happens if they take action.

Salespeople often naturally procrastinate when it comes to such things as paperwork. One salesperson never submitted expense vouchers because he couldn't be bothered filling out the reports—he preferred to just pay the expenses out of his own pocket. Actually, depending on the expenses involved, he might have been better off not spending the time to submit the report, but I suspect that over time these expenses added up to thousands of dollars in travel-related and client-related expenses. A better alternative could have been to have someone else do them.

While not submitting expense reports can affect the salesperson's bottom line from the expense side, not doing a good job at market development will affect the revenue side. This can spell the difference between success and failure.

Prospecting and cold calling are two activities that can be put off for a variety of reasons:

- It's not the right time
- No good list to work from
- Too much paperwork involved in followup
- Too busy taking care of current business
- Fear of rejection
- Fear of acceptance (having to do the work and to prove oneself)

It seems easier and more productive to develop more work with existing customers than spend time developing new customers, but the problem is that you *will* experience customer turnover. Customers move to different jobs, retire, or decide to use different suppliers. Companies are bought out, and new management often has preferred suppliers.

Keeping new customers in the pipeline is the only way to ensure viability. Besides keeping your pipeline full, prospecting and cold calling allow you to shape your business by targeting your efforts at those customers who best fit your customer profile.

> *"You're not going to keep a pipeline full by waiting for customers to call."*
> —Ray Reisert Jr., president, PW Funding

True procrastinators can always find a reason to put off what they are supposed to do. When people procrastinate, they are not putting off low-value projects. That is good time management. Rather, they are putting off things they know they should or must do: things that will add value to their work or personal lives or things that will diminish worry.

What are the consequences of procrastination?

- Lost income
- Worry and distraction
- Lost time and energy
- Lost opportunities
- Diminished self-esteem

When you tackle the things you fear the most, you grow personally and enhance self-esteem. When you procrastinate, you are still doing the thing you are putting off. How? You are doing it over and over in your mind. I can attest to this with a personal example. One time my electric garage door opener broke. I went out right away to replace it with a new one. I brought it home and opened up the boxes. The installation instructions were on a multipanel foldout with diagrams, arrows, letters, and numbers. I looked at it and said, "I don't want to read this right now. I'll do it later." Three months later, I still hadn't installed it. But winter was approaching, and I knew if I didn't get it done now I would soon have to get into a cold car each day. When I opened the boxes and placed the parts on the floor, I had a great sense of relief.

Every day during those three months I had been thinking about installing the garage door opener. Every time I walked by the garage, every time I went into the garage, every time I had to open the garage door by hand, it was on my mind. When I finally began the job of installation, I felt relieved. It took less than two hours to complete, but I had spent even more time thinking and worrying about doing it.

"It takes more energy to think about something than it does to do it."
—Evelyn Jordan, mom

Market Development

Whether you call it *prospecting* or *business development* or *market development*, to be successful as a sales professional, we know we must develop a constant supply of new customers. Why? Even if you have a base of repeat customers you can rely on for steady business, customers move on. People change jobs, companies have budget cutbacks or go out of business. What is the turnover in your customer base from year to year? Would it be safe to assume 10 to 20 percent? If so, you need to add one to two new customers for every ten existing customers just to stay even.

Developing your potential market is a lot like developing muscles: it takes effort, it takes stretching, and it doesn't happen by sitting on the sidelines and waiting for the phone to ring.

Here's something I hate to admit: by nature, I'm a procrastinator. I have to be extra disciplined in certain areas to avoid procrastinating (one of the philosophies I use to get things done is to "Do it Now.") One activity I have a tendency to put off, and it is a critical one, is prospecting and cold calling. Not that I can't do these things and not that I don't enjoy doing them when I do them. But I prefer working with clients as opposed to finding them. I like the conceptual challenge of designing a training, speaking, or organizational solution for a client, and this is where my expertise is greatest. But I know enough to supplement my own efforts at finding clients with those of others. I also reach out to prospective new clients by such vehicles as writing articles and referrals. If you are like me at all, you'll need to be extra disciplined in certain activities that you know you need to do to be successful but don't find as enjoyable as certain other activities.

I've found it easy to invent ways to avoid prospecting and cold calling. For me the most common technique is to stay busy with other relevant business activities, such as taking care of existing business. This offers the convenient excuse to avoid picking up the phone. To stop procrastinating, schedule a set time or times to get on the phone.

Back up your phone time with advanced marketing strategies. Decide whom your best customer prospects are, describe what you have to offer them that is unique and gives them results they want, and then look for creative ways to grab their attention and stand out from the crowd to get noticed, such as writing articles.

How do you expand your customer base? Prospecting, cold calling, referrals, and mailings are the most common ways that sales professionals reach out to new customers. Support your efforts with other techniques, such as advertising or publicity, news releases, articles, and seminars.

Create Momentum

Steven Spielberg once remarked, "The faster I work, the better I work." He said that when he is making a movie, the quicker he can get it done, the easier it is for him to see how it is coming together. When he can start to see several scenes at one time and they are fresh in his mind, he has a better idea of where he needs to go. When I said this to a group of salespeople as part of a presentation on value, a number of them shook their heads in agreement.

When it comes to cold calling, it also pays to work quicker and to create momentum. It's not likely you're going to get much in the way of results from making an isolated call. But when you make calls consistently, over time you will start to see results. As you see those results, they reinforce the importance of making more calls. Success builds on itself.

The more people you are in front of, the more opportunities you'll have. Keep getting in front of people and you will find those who need and want what you have to offer. Your marketing efforts to make yourself known will pay off. It's a matter of finding the right customers, and the more customers you are in front of, the greater the chance you have of finding the right ones.

Three Steps to Overcoming Procrastination

- Realize that you pay a dear price when you put things off: worry. When you do the thing right away, the worry goes away.
- Because one of the reasons people procrastinate is perfectionism, practice every day doing one small thing that can be done incorrectly without consequences, such as placing a stamp on an envelope crooked.
- Do it now! Just get started. Take the first step! Once you've mastered this, the second step will come more easily.

Choices

Our lives are the sum of the choices we make. When you are presented with the opportunity to choose, choose thoughtfully.

The Power of Control

It's not what happens to us. It's how we react to it.

One of the most powerful theories of human performance is a model developed by Albert Ellis, founder of the Albert Ellis Institute. He proposed, based on the observations of such influential thinkers as the philosopher Epictetus (who said, "Men are not influenced by things, but by their thoughts about things"), that our emotional state isn't determined as much by what happens to us as it is by how we react to what happens to us. He also proposed that there are more constructive and less constructive reactions. To "awfulize" things, or say they shouldn't be the way they are and become anxious or depressed as a result of those events, is ineffectual and unnecessary. There are alternatives and we have the ability to choose them.

For example, suppose you lose a big sale. You could become distressed and let that distract you from your future actions. Or you could be disappointed but relatively quickly move beyond that disappointment and even learn from what happened. You have the choice; people who move ahead move beyond disappointment. What usually holds people back in this type of situation is not competence, but attitude. The wrong attitude can keep you from getting the sale.

Here is one of the great lessons I've learned. We always have a choice about how to react to a situation. When I look back at the people I worked for, I remember some managers who knew how to manage and some who didn't. When I worked for the people who managed well, people who explained what they wanted and gave autonomy and trusted me to do my job, I responded with my best work. When I worked for managers who criticized, played games, or played favorites, I found it hard to maintain that same level of commitment or performance. Why would the same person respond so differently in these two situations? Part of it was that so much of how I viewed myself was tied up in who I was on the *job*.

What I've learned by reflecting on those types of situations is that there are ways to make the best of a bad situation. Here are my suggestions for doing that.

- Use better interpersonal skills to encourage better relationships.
- Consider the boss to be your client and seek to meet his or her requirements, no matter how difficult they may be.
- Separate yourself from your job. Your value as a person doesn't depend on your job performance. If your job performance is good, be glad about it. If it needs improvement, be confident and seek to improve it. Don't let someone else's evaluation of your performance, whether good or bad, affect your evaluation of yourself as a person.

The danger in circumstances such as these is fear rooted in past experiences. If you can keep yourself from activating those fears in the first place, you can have better control over your perception of the situation. One of the things you can do when you find yourself in situations that remind you of times when you weren't at your best is to think about times when you were. Instead of dwelling on how you ran into problems, recall those times when you overcame problems. You have a choice about what to think, so why not think about something positive?

Make a Choice: Better or Bitter

I heard a woman say one time after she had lived through a terrible experience that she knew that she could get either better or bitter from it. When you are faced with a similar situation, try to remember that the choice is yours. Holding on to bitterness doesn't change the situation for the better. Getting better does. Taking positive action does.

Don't Hold Grudges

Grudges take a tremendous amount of energy. They take your focus off more constructive efforts. In a business setting, they will diminish or destroy your ability to function effectively and will close off future opportunities. Why? Grudges are infectious to you and the people around you, so people try to avoid the combatants. Instead of holding on to a grudge, let go. Move on. There are many ways you can choose to let go. However you decide to do it, you will be a better person for it. You will be looking toward the future, not living in the past. You will find your energy level restored. And you will feel excited about your renewed outlook.

Choose Your Boss Wisely

Think twice about the person you choose to work for, if you are given a choice in the matter. No one in the workplace will ever have as much influence over your success as does the person you work for.

I wish I had known a long time ago what I know now about how important it is to think about the person you work for. I have worked for a dozen or so different people. Of those dozen, about three quarters of them were good to work for. Several were really good to work for. And then there were three people I should have known more about before I went to work for them. The jobs I went into were good, but in these cases I wasn't well matched with the person I worked for.

You are the person responsible for your career. The person you work for is going to be instrumental in helping you to achieve your career goals. Not that you can't achieve those goals in spite of that person, or that you can't learn lessons from that person. But if you have a choice, choose a boss who is capable, honest, supportive, and respected by colleagues, bosses, or customers. Consider the person you work for just as you consider the job itself. It will make your life easier and may help keep your career on a fast track.

State of Mind

Think of a business situation you've been in that was unpleasant or unsuccessful. Now think about a business situation you've been in that was pleasant and led to success. Think about how that situation felt.

Did you notice your jaw clench up a bit when you recalled the unpleasant situation? Did you start to stare at an object? Did you feel a sense of letdown? Did you notice yourself relaxing a bit when recalling the pleasant experience, perhaps smile just a little and feel a sense of a well-being?

All of us have had both unpleasant and pleasant experiences. Recognizing what could be done better the next time we find ourselves in those types of situations and then moving on is the lesson to take away. Facing a challenging situation by thinking about a successful past situation predisposes us to more success.

A Cure for Worry

Worrying is a waste of energy. When we worry, we get distracted. We can even lose sleep. The problem is, nothing changes when we worry.

The cure for worrying is to start planning and take action. Analyze the situation—identify your alternatives and the pros and cons of each—and develop a plan of action. Realize that no plan is perfect, so build in contingencies: What if A, B, or C happens? What will you do? Plan for that contingency now.

When you have a plan in place and have taken decisive action, stop worrying. Either what you feared will not come to pass because of the actions you have taken, or it will, and you will be as prepared as you can be for that possibility. In the meantime, you will have gained peace of mind. You will have more energy. You will have been able to focus on other important priorities. And you will have less to worry about!

Change

Our ability to change is limited only by our willingness to do so and by our discomfort with not doing so.

Unconscious Competence

Have you ever taught someone how to drive? Was it someone close to you? How easy was it? It is often difficult and frustrating. The primary reason it is difficult is that as an experienced driver, you do so many things automatically when you drive that you expect the person you are teaching to do the same. Of course, when you give control of the steering, braking, and acceleration to the other person, you feel more uncomfortable.

One day I was in the car with one of my daughters, who was practicing after she got her learner's permit. As she made a U-turn too quickly for my comfort, I reacted instinctively, moving my hand up as I motioned to her to make sure she was going to stop. Of course, she knew enough to stop and felt as if I didn't trust her. What was second nature to me was a challenge for her. For new drivers, there is so much to concentrate on that it is hard for them to keep track of everything that experienced drivers take for granted.

When we perform and execute without thinking about it, we're operating on a level called *unconscious competence*. Most times that doesn't present a problem. When things such as technology change, we may try doing things the way we've always done them and find it doesn't work. If we want to learn, we need to drop into *conscious competence*, a state in which we think about what we're doing. In that state of competence, we are alert and less prone to making mistakes. Just like the new driver who is careful to come to a complete stop at a stop sign (instead of a rolling stop), we sometimes need to get back to the fine points that made us successful in the first place.

All of us have blind spots, things we are unaware of about ourselves that other people *are* aware of. Typically, blind spots refer to problem areas, but they may also refer to strengths.

A client asked me to work with him on project management. I've worked on many projects, including many large ones, and as I reflected on what I would need to design, I thought to myself that project management wasn't that hard. But then I realized that I was unconsciously competent about project management. I did things I had learned from the experience of many projects and didn't realize what was really involved. I had to step back into a conscious competence pattern and think about what makes a successful project.

Intellectual Depreciation

I was stopped one day at a stoplight and happened to look over at the outside of a restaurant. The paint was peeling and the building was in need of general maintenance. Buildings deteriorate. As a matter of fact, the tax codes allow businesses to deduct an expense called *depreciation*. It recognizes that buildings and other capital goods lose value.

It occurred to me that knowledge operates by the same principle. All knowledge has a limited "shelf life." Knowledge deteriorates. It must be maintained.

Intellectual capital describes what is in the mind of a person. The most valuable assets an organization or an individual can have are knowledge and the will to succeed. Protecting intellectual capital means continually striving to learn and update knowledge.

There is *tacit knowledge* and *explicit knowledge*. Tacit knowledge is what resides in our minds. Explicit knowledge is what has been written down or formalized in some way so that others have convenient access to it. Find the tacit knowledge by talking with others. Develop a process for passing along knowledge that you or your sales colleagues develop. Take advantage of what people learn to let it benefit others.

To be an exceptional sales leader, you'll want to constantly scan available sources of information for new ideas, trends, problems, and opportunities. Continually look for ways to update your knowledge and skills to be current with the latest technology. Success hinges on your ability to access information and put it to productive use. It also depends on your ability to stay ahead of your competition when it comes to taking advantage of new knowledge, technology, or customer needs. Don't get caught in the trap of thinking that you have all the answers. The smarter you are, the more questions you have and the more you know you need to learn.

La Trobe University has a French motto, *Qui cherche trouve*, which means, "Whoever seeks shall find." When we're confronted with evidence that there are things we could or should do differently, our natural defensive reaction is to believe that we don't need to change. Yet, if we look for ways to improve, we'll find them. The exceptional leader is open to change. Sometimes my own defensive reaction when presented with something different is to say, "I know that." Then I remember that I don't know everything. No one does.

One time I was in a taxi coming home from the airport. Many times I need to give drivers more information than just the address for them to find my home. On this trip, the driver took a route that was different from the one that most drivers take. When he got to a certain point, I suggested he turn on 162nd Street, thinking that he wasn't familiar with the area. He said he was going to turn on 158th Street. He asked me if I knew that this street had only one light, while 162nd Street had several. It was quicker, he said. As soon as he said he was turning on 158th, I thought, "I've lived here for many years and I know this area." But I realized that even though I had lived in the area for many years, there was still something I could learn about it. I didn't know every street. He traveled these streets every day, all day. More than what I learned about a particular street that day, I understood better than before that no one can know everything.

In my workshops, I say that one of my objectives is to have participants learn from each other because everyone has lived unique experiences. So the next time you find yourself reactively thinking, "I don't need to know that," ask yourself if it's really true.

I have found that sales leaders are receptive to learning. You would think it would be just the opposite. You would think that it would be the new salespeople who would soak up information. But sales leaders are sales leaders because they never cease to look for ways to do things better. They have a large experience base and know what works and what doesn't. It's refreshing to work with individuals who approach learning in this way.

Learn Something New with Every Sale

No matter what happens with every sale you are involved with, take the opportunity to learn something new. Gain some new industry knowledge, ask a new question, or discover a new way of presenting the high-value benefits your services and products deliver to customers. Learn why the customer didn't buy. Improve your questioning skills, your presentation skills, or your understanding of the customer's buying style. On a larger sale, it could be how the bid was developed or how it was presented. There is always something to learn when it comes to skills.

Let's return for a moment to attitude. If you can live through a difficult situation, you can almost always learn from it. This is true even if what you had to live through was embarrassing, degrading, or life threatening, and it is true regardless of whether what happened was caused by someone else or by you. The fact that you endured is a tribute to your courage. If you can step away from what happened and find the lessons that it presents to you, that is also a tribute to your courage. It takes courage to survive. It's easier to grab on to bitterness, resentment, or fear—after all, doing this gives us someone or something else to blame. But the decision to hold on to that resentment is yours, and so is the decision to let it go. Your freedom to make that decision is one of the greatest freedoms you possess. Never let someone take it from you. Never surrender it.

Habits Are Hard to Change

Have you ever moved a piece of furniture to a different location, only to continue going to the old spot, expecting it to be there? Even though you know consciously that the furniture is in the new location, your habit of going to the old location is still operational. Habits save us time. We don't need to think about things that don't have much consequence. From that viewpoint, habits are helpful. On the other hand, unproductive habits keep us stuck. Once habits are formed, they are hard to break.

When you want to change a habit, you must first make a conscious decision to do so. Then you need to follow through on that decision. The following three suggestions come from well-known psychologist William James, who stated that following through on a decision required self-discipline and believed that three steps were essential to making the change endure once you decide to do it.

- Act at the first *opportunity*.
- Start out *strong*.
- Don't let an *exception* occur.

Act at the first opportunity once you have made a decision to do something—that is when your motivation is the greatest it is ever going to be. The more you delay, the less likely it is that you are going to do what you planned.

I have what I call the *half-life theory of motivation*: A day after you have made a decision to do something, your motivation will be half of what it was when you made the decision. The next day it will be half again. So in a matter of a couple of days, if you haven't done what you decided to do, you won't do it. That's why you'll want to act at the first opportunity once you've made a decision.

Starting out strong means overcompensating. You need to aim to do more than you would like to so that if you don't quite get to the level you were working for, you will still make your goal.

Don't let an exception occur, because if you do it is easy to fall back into the old habit. If an exception does occur, it doesn't mean you should abandon your original goal. Instead, recognize the progress you have made and recommit to your goal.

"To thrive on change, you must understand how to give in to it, flow with it, and derive strength from it."

—Michael Dell, CEO, Dell Computer

When we have positive habits, we sometimes drift away from them. For example, you may have attended seminars or conferences periodically to keep up to date in your field, but may now find yourself attending fewer events like these. Many people resolutely start an exercise program or diet, only to find their determination diminishing slowly over time.

When you find your resolve flagging, recommit to your original goals. Recall the positive benefits you originally felt and the resolve you once had. It is natural to require reinforcement to maintain your motivation.

What Works at Work Won't Necessarily Work at Home

A majority of salespeople are to the point, fast paced, and results oriented. Those qualities tend to serve them well in the work environment. However, at home it may be a different story. Imagine that one spouse is trying to describe to the other some events that took place that day. The results-oriented spouse says, "Is there a point to this?" Of course, the spouse who was relating the events wasn't exactly looking for that type of response.

I don't know about you, but I find the issues that I face at work are easier to manage than the issues I face at home, even considering the complicated dynamics that take place in the typical work organization. I think the challenge at home arises from the intensity of feelings we have with people we live with and our expectations of them.

A big part of the challenge we face is that when we are at work we have to be "on" all the time. That takes energy. So when we get home, we want to unwind and relax. While we may be constrained in how we handle ourselves at work, we may feel we have more freedom at home to say what's on our mind or do what we really feel like doing. We expect others to understand.

Of course, the people you live with deserve to be treated as tactfully as the people you work with. The reality is that they are more important to you than your work colleagues, even though they willingly accept the sacrifices you make at work. Unfortunately, you can't behave exactly the same way at work and at home. The expectations aren't the same, and neither are the expected outcomes.

So what is the answer? If we can't simply use the same behaviors at work that make us successful there and can't just unwind and be ourselves at home, what should we do? The answer lies in understanding human behavior. To be successful, stop focusing solely on what you want and how you feel and instead factor in a response to the other person. In other words, give that person what he or she needs or wants in the way he or she prefers it. If this sounds familiar, it is. It is exactly what the most successful salespeople do for their customers.

The most successful salespeople reach out to customers and extend themselves to make sure customers get what they want in the way they want it. The salesperson who discounts what customers value, doesn't listen, or even argues with customers isn't going to get the sale or keep the relationship for long. Even if the salesperson is right, it won't matter.

So why should the situation be any different at home? Why shouldn't you treat the people who mean the most to you at least as respectfully as you treat your customers? Why not consider your family to be another group of customers, just under a different set of circumstances? Do you think that might change the dynamics in the relationship? This might involve going outside of your preferred mode of behaviors, but it will likely result in your preferred outcomes.

Why is it easier to see the mistakes that other people make and the problems that other people have than it is to see our own? The answer is not simple. Being too close to a problem emotionally, or too afraid to admit a mistake, may make it impossible to see your situation in the same way that others do. Once I was listening to some people talk about problems they were facing, and it seemed so obvious to me what they should do to resolve the problems. I thought, "Why don't they just do it?" But when I happened to describe a problem I was having, even though it was almost the same as the ones that I had heard other people describe, the answer didn't seem so obvious.

My wife, Terry, who has a lot of wisdom about people, gave me an idea about how to handle these personal situations one time when I was perplexed about what I should do. She said, "If one of your clients approached you with the same problem, what would you tell them to do? Do whatever you would have told them to do."

Warren Bennis, a professor and author, told a story at a conference about how he had difficulty deciding whether to accept an offer to teach at another university. He went to a colleague and explained the situation. The colleague said, "Warren, you're the expert on decision making. Why don't you follow your own model?" Warren said he told him, "This is too important. This is about me!"

Always Go Forward

It is often tempting to return to the familiar and the comfortable. We reminisce about how good something was or how we would like to find that special time again. In business, we sometimes would like things to be the way they were in earlier times, when they were less complicated. Sometimes we like to revisit a past problem we already solved. (It's like seeing a movie for a second time. You know the outcome.) This may be gratifying, but if we have moved beyond the level where we were, we may regress to a level we no longer want to be at. Instead, look for new challenges that will stretch you beyond your present level of performance.

Career Advice

A veteran salesperson once told me that when he started his career, his sales manager gave him advice that he has lived by:

- Work for a leader.
- Tell the truth.
- Get them to like you.

These are simple truths that make sense. No matter what stage you are at in your career, whether you are just beginning or are a veteran, it pays to think about your career direction and goals. If you don't do it, who will? If you don't do it, how will you know what you want and get it?

In an interview on "Inside the Actors Studio," Stockard Channing said that on five occasions she had accepted movies solely for the money, and they turned out to be bad movies. She quoted someone who said there are three reasons to take a job: to make money, to advance your career, or to learn something. "Go for at least two" was the advice she said was worth following.

Kathy Egan is vice president of sales at Olympic Management, a hotel property management company located in Buffalo that is just completing four record-setting quarters at a time when many others aren't meeting last year's numbers. She has five strategies for success that she shared with me:

- *Develop relationships.* Kathy advises her salespeople to really get to know people: "Close your laptop, stand up, and go meet people." She believes that establishing a relationship with a potential client gives a salesperson a big advantage over someone who wants to sell the client something without first establishing that relationship. Besides, she notes, "It's a lot harder to say no to someone face to face!"

- *Personalize the relationship.* Kathy also believes that "the more people tech up, the more important it is to personalize the customer relationship, whether it's through a handshake or a handwritten note." Kathy doesn't send form letters; she doesn't think people like receiving them or that they keep them. If someone is a past customer, she sees it as a no-brainer to send a note.

- *Stay in touch with customers.* Kathy's group writes a little note to those people who are not booked at the beginning of the year: "We noticed that you haven't rebooked. The dates are still available, so give us a call when you're ready." She says they'll save the note, though they won't save a form letter. "I'm not talking about cold calling. What I'm referring to is contacting people who've either been referred to us or who've done business with us."

- *Look for opportunities, even in adversity.* When businesspeople cut back travel, Kathy had a focused effort to contact meeting planners to let them know about her nearby property. As a result, her property generated an extra $100,000 in bookings at a time when business was down for most. Her group tries many different tactics and then zooms in on what works. If an industry segment is picking up, they ask existing customers, "Whom should we be calling on?"

- *Put your time to good use.* Kathy believes that her salespeople shouldn't waste time going after "little fish" when they could be using that time to go after the big ones. She also believes that if the customer doesn't respond after repeated attempts, it's time to move on. "Some people have a hard time letting go. There's a value on your time. The time a salesperson invests should be at least equal to the return he or she can expect." See people face to face.

Salespeople can't afford to be busy but not productive. Kathy notes, "It's easy to get caught up in the wrong things." Many salespeople say that theirs is a relationship business. The earlier you develop those relationships and the more you nurture them, the stronger the relationships will be, and the more they will result in business. Positive relationships can lead to impressive results.

Become an Expert

Become an expert in your field of business. Take it beyond being an expert about your industry. Become an expert about a certain type of problem. Talk to people who have experience in the area. Read everything you can on the subject. Develop a theory about the problem: When is it most likely to happen? What causes it? What can be done about it? Become an expert in the subtle differences between it and similar problems. Become an expert on trends in your industry and profession. Learn about technology that is changing business processes.

I am not suggesting that you become an expert in every facet of the sales process. But make the customer the focus. Start by looking at what you do almost effortlessly, well enough to take it for granted. You are probably unconsciously competent about it. Maybe it is how to influence others. Step back and look at what you do that allows you to be so effective. Ask others for their opinions about it. Build on that skill.

When you become an expert, write articles that can be published in industry publications. You can provide examples of what you have done (keep the company names anonymous unless you get the company's written permission). The article should provide helpful advice and shouldn't come across as a sales promotion.

Write about the symptoms of a common sales problem, how people can assess whether they have this problem, and the consequences of not fixing it. Describe in general terms what it takes to fix the problem.

In most cases, you should check with your manager to be sure your company supports the article. At the very least, try to get the article published in your company's in-house publication, if one exists. Be sure that you don't reveal confidential or proprietary information. Check with your legal department if you have a concern in that area.

When the article is published, get reprints. Get it on your company's Web site, if possible. Being published in this way allows you to be recognized as a leader in your field.

Do you have aspirations to move up into management? If so, what are your motives for doing so? Recognize that the responsibilities of a sales manager require a different set of skills than those of a salesperson. Moving into management means that you will work primarily through your salespeople and that your success depends on their success. Typically, your responsibilities for direct selling will be limited. Communication, coaching, and leadership are some of the skills you will need to rely on as a sales manager. You will build on some of the skills you used as a salesperson, such as your ability to plan and organize, but those play a secondary role.

If you aspire to become a manager, first examine whether it is something you will enjoy doing. Second, determine the extent to which you have demonstrated the skills needed to succeed as a manager. Third, when you are promoted into management, develop a plan for improving the skills you need to be successful at that level. Finally, be cautious of gravitating into those areas in which you are most familiar and most comfortable: selling. If you go on a sales call with a salesperson, be there to coach, not to sell.

It is much better to move into a higher-level position aware of what the requirements are than to discover them when you get there. Do what you enjoy and learn to do it well.

"Don't Take This Personally"

What do you do when someone says "Don't take this personally" to you? Most likely, you take it personally. Apply this quick test to tell whether the statement is actually personal: ask yourself, *Would this be happening to just about anyone else in this situation?* If the answer is yes, it isn't personal. For example, if a customer is screaming at you about a product that isn't working properly, that isn't personal. He or she would more than likely scream at any company representative. On the other hand, if the product wasn't the right one for the job and you sold it, it more than likely is personal.

What difference does it make whether it is personal? If you know the customer's displeasure isn't with you, it allows you to be more objective. You can handle the problem without being a part of the problem. As a result, you can usually help the customer better.

What do you do if it *is* personal, if there is some criticism of you in the customer's or colleague's complaint? Listen, understand, and consider whether you need to do something differently in the future. The information you are receiving may be valuable if you can act on it.

Sales leaders don't take rejection personally. They may not accept it, but they are resilient enough to use it to their advantage and learn from it.

"You've got to make your own life. You can't be swayed by people telling you no."
—Danny DeVito, actor

Communication

Your technical skills and product knowledge may play a crucial role in your ability to be successful as a salesperson. Really good communication skills are essential for every salesperson. Communication is the lifeline of success.

Communication involves both giving information and listening. It is both speaking and writing. It is both a skill and an attitude. It affects both business and personal success. Everyone can improve communication skills, even people who are already skilled communicators.

Everyone can find ways to listen better. Everyone can find ways to present information better. Everyone can find ways to use words that convey meaning more effectively, words that awaken senses or evoke emotions. Everyone can find ways to inspire others through their words. Everyone can find ways to improve tone of voice and diction. (Think of actors whose trademark voices make them immediately recognizable.) Everyone can improve written communications by making them more succinct, less confusing, or more motivational.

Communication is a skill that we rarely learn in formal education to the extent we need it. Most of us will learn the most about writing, followed by speaking, with listening a distant third. I've asked thousands of people whether they have ever taken a listening course, and I would say less than a dozen people have ever answered affirmatively. Yet that is probably the most critical of the three. So the one we need to rely on the most and the one that is critical to our success is often the one we are the least prepared for.

Take the Lead

Continually look for ways to improve the way you communicate. Ask for feedback from people you work with every day and from those you come into contact with occasionally or even once. Ask someone whose judgment and honesty you can trust to help you gain an objective view of your strengths and where you need to improve. Have this person listen to one of your presentations. Ask him or her for feedback in specific areas. Don't react defensively if he or she tells you something you weren't prepared to hear. Evaluate whether it is valid and then act on any valid points.

On a personal level, relationships succeed when people can communicate. Being able to do that when faced with all of the emotions and history inherent in relationships is an enormous challenge. It's important to always practice tact, honesty, and sincerity.

Resolve to Become a Better Listener

The most effective salespeople listen really well. In the selling process, listening helps you gather information, build trust, and confirm the customer's expectations. If you restate, summarize, and empathize with what the customer has told you, you will move toward closure. It becomes a part of the decision-making process.

Do you know something you could be doing to be more effective? Why would you say you *aren't* doing it? Probably habits are to blame. Listening is a skill that can always be improved, and it is critically important for sales leaders.

The Most Successful Salespeople

The most successful salespeople get in step with the customer. If the customer wants to move at a quicker pace (which is the pace that most salespeople would prefer), they move at a quicker pace. If the customer wants to move at a more deliberate pace, the salesperson also moves at a more deliberate pace, even if this is not what the salesperson would prefer to do. If the customer wants to get right down to business, the salesperson does too, instead of commenting on what's in the person's office, for example. If the customer wants to chat for a bit, the salesperson chats for a bit (but not indefinitely).

Go with the flow. If you try to rush customers who want to analyze the data, they'll go even slower because they will feel compelled to tell you why they need more time to analyze the information or make a decision. If you continue to press them for a decision, they will avoid making any decision or will simply tell you no. The more impatient you get, the longer the sale will take or the less likely it is that you will even get it. Unless customers are willing to adapt, they won't go at your pace. You need to adapt to theirs. If you want to get along with the variety of customers you meet, be open to working in the way they prefer to work. You will find that they will be more receptive to your recommendations.

Don't Jump to a Conclusion

It is easy to judge people by misinterpreting their behavior. When a customer doesn't return a call, you might think that it is for a variety of plausible reasons: he or she is busy, preoccupied, working on a new project, or out of the office unexpectedly. You might wonder whether he or she is reluctant to talk with you, doesn't want to be bothered, or didn't like what you had to say before. Any of those explanations may be right, or they may be wrong. You don't know for sure unless the customer tells you. They only thing you know for sure is that the customer didn't return the call.

When you misinterpret someone's behavior, you can unwittingly set the stage for an unfortunate sequence of events. You can think negatively and undermine your ability to be successful. Or you can communicate something that is wrong to the customer because of your misinterpretation.

Understanding the difference between behavior and how we judge that behavior is one of the most enlightening things that one can learn. Why? Because failing to discern the difference is the root of so much ill will. It's common for people to observe someone's behavior and assume the person's motivation for the behavior. But the motivation may be entirely different from what an observer would assume. If the observer were to communicate with that person based on his or her assumptions, the person might well react negatively to the presumption, which then leads to further negative reactions from both parties.

It is so easy to misinterpret people's behavior. One day, I had just pulled out of a service station after getting gas. I was waiting at the light and noticed the man in the car behind me when I looked in my rear-view mirror. When the light turned green, he pulled out quickly from behind me to the right side and I thought he was accelerating to cut in front of me, so I accelerated. He accelerated more and so did I, until we got to the light at the next intersection, whereupon he rolled down his window and told me that the gas cap was on the car. "Thank you," I replied.

The reason that people misjudge others' behaviors is those behaviors trigger emotions based on our experiences in similar situations. If you had a negative experience in a past similar situation, you might expect to have a negative experience in this circumstance as well and react accordingly. Of course, while the behavior may be similar, the reason behind it can be very different.

Behavior is what someone says or does. We observe behavior through our eyes or ears, but we judge behavior in our minds. That is where we decide whether we like it or don't like it. That is where we decide whether we need to be careful. That is where we react emotionally—and if that reaction is negative, it can cloud our thinking and our response. No one wins in this situation.

During a listening exercise in a program I recently did, one of the participants was supposed to just listen to his partner tell him about a little problem he was having at work. The person who was listening asked the speaker whether what he did was his responsibility. The speaker reacted negatively to the question. I believe he reacted negatively because he may have interpreted the question as a challenge. It was a simple question, but the fact that it was asked, or perhaps how it was asked, led to a negative interaction between these two people.

What would have been better? Perhaps the listener should not have asked the question, or explained that he simply wanted to understand this person's responsibilities better. Perhaps the speaker could simply have answered the question, or, if he didn't want to get sidetracked in the discussion, asked the person to hold the question.

It isn't that we should not have reactions to what people say or do. We merely need to be clear about the difference between what we see and hear and our *interpretations* of what we see and hear. If we communicate with people more about their behavior, they will have a less defensive response. As a result, our communication will lead to the results we want more often.

Bob Felekey is a twenty-five-year veteran who's handled a variety of complex sales in international situations. Based on his experience, he has evolved five principles for creating winning sales.

- Understand your strategic advantages. Ask, "What resources do we have that the competition doesn't?" Use those resources to your advantage.
- Extend the "buying circle" by working with other suppliers and alliance partners. If the customer has tested or implemented a product or service from a noncompetitive supplier, partner with them and demonstrate that you complement decisions the customer has already made. Blend in and add value to their process.
- Talk to the person whose career depends on making the right decision and who will be emotionally involved in using the product.

- Be responsive to the cultural customs of your customers. Understand where the other person is coming from and be ready to do what makes them comfortable.
- Don't get burned by giving away the solution, only to have the customer shop the lowest price.

Make the Most of Your Achievements

"You Can't Buy Happiness"

New research by Dr. Richard Ryan, professor of psychology at the University of Rochester, and Dr. Tim Kasser is showing that people whose primary focus is on money, fame, or beauty tend to be more depressed and have more "behavioral" problems and physical discomfort. People who primarily want to develop close relationships, become more self-aware, or contribute to the community tend to be happier. The key words are *primary focus*.

They also found that extrinsic satisfactions such as wealth, beauty, and fame don't have to result in dissatisfaction. But it appears that if we achieve those without a meaningful balance in our relationships, growth, or contribution to others, we tend to feel unfulfilled.

Is it because wealth, beauty, and fame are a bit like cotton candy—sweet and fluffy but lacking substance? Is it because they don't relate to our humanness? What does your experience tell you?

> *"Happiness is having the freedom to be yourself."*
> —Hilary Swank, actor

Have You Achieved the Level of Success You Believe You're Capable Of?

There are few limits to what we can do. I read an interesting story about an eighty-five-year-old woman who was a member of a reading group and was also writing a novel. After being turned down by a number of publishers, she found one who was willing to publish her book, which turned into a bestseller. She went on to write two others.

Age can work against us, but it can also work for us. If you are young, you bring fresh ideas. If you are older, you bring wisdom. In the same way, education might or might not help. Being perceptive, effective, or intelligent doesn't require education. What it does require is an understanding of human nature, an open mind, and, often, a sense of humor or an ability to not take ourselves too seriously regardless of how seriously we take our work. There is little that really stands in our way— only that which we allow. Everyone has challenges. It could be time constraints due to family commitments. It could be financial constraints. Those challenges may mean it will take you longer to do what you want to do, but they don't have to mean that you won't do it.

> *"Achievement seemed to be a double-edged sword for me. I had a subconscious feeling that triumph would always bring a loss. I realized that what was limiting me was the residual pain associated with accomplishment."*
>
> —Sela Ward, actor

Greatness Lies Within Each of Us

I don't believe that achieving greatness is about money or position, or even about fame or recognition for accomplishments. I believe that we have the opportunity to achieve greatness when we touch the lives of others. We can do that through our actions and words. We can do it at work and at home. People who accumulate great wealth are remembered for their wealth. But what makes them special is the good they choose to do with their money.

Most people who reach the end of their lives don't think, "I wish I could make one more sale"—or work on one more project or make more money. Most of us would think more about the people we love than the work we didn't get done. Yet it is easy to lose track of what is really important. If someone were to ask you to rank, in order of priority, yourself, your career, and your family, in what order would you place them?

Most people tend to put career first, followed by family, followed by self. Yet if we don't take care of ourselves first, how can we take care of our families, our careers, or anything else? There is no right or wrong when you think about these priorities. It is more a matter of balance. We start to run into difficulties when we get out of balance.

Salespeople can be highly dedicated to their work and their clients. Their work may entail being on call, traveling, or extended hours. Families are often asked to understand and sacrifice, and most times they will—as long as there is a balance. Salespeople have asked me about that balance. They want to know how to better manage their time so they can satisfy not only their clients but their loved ones as well. The bottom line is that if we make all the sacrifices for the job but don't keep the balance with our families, what is the point of the sacrifice? When the job is done, what will you have left? Effective leaders know that they need to plan out their schedules, set boundaries around their availability, and plan time with the people they love.

In one session I facilitated, I had two successful salespeople. One planned vacations for his family. The other never found the time, and his wife wasn't happy about it. As we talked about it, he realized it was time for him to adjust the way he planned his work schedule and family time. His family was always coming in second.

During another sales workshop, one of the people said that as a result of the time he spent on the job he rarely saw his children. On the other hand, I read a story about a fellow who planned his schedule around his children's. He said that when their school calendars came out he would write their events in his calendar and, to the extent that he could, work around them. He said that if something was scheduled on one of those days, he might be late to a meeting or to a business dinner that conflicted with their performances. He said he tries "like crazy" to be home for dinner by being in the car when six o'clock rolls around. He leaves early in the morning. He said if people ask him to dinner, he says he can do breakfast or lunch. He said he had "only a few years to be part of their lives."

I try to take whatever opportunities I have to spend time with my daughters—even if it's just something like driving them to school or taking them to an appointment. I could feel guilty about not doing work during that time, but these occasions don't happen that often, and I don't know how long I will have these opportunities.

Success is achieving goals. Greatness is more than fame. Greatness is touching the essence of the human spirit in meaningful and lasting ways. Every day we have the opportunity to pass along good things or bad things. Whatever we pass along is going to be given by that person to someone else. Which do you prefer to choose?

Have No Regrets

During a commercial for an auto manufacturer, the announcers interviewed two people about regrets. They say they don't have any until he reveals a secret one has kept from the other. It's funny. But the reality is that it's difficult when a good relationship ends in a bad way.

Don't let a relationship end on a note of regret. Every day we are given the opportunity to change course. Do what you need to today, because you don't know whether you will be given the opportunity tomorrow.

> *"I sacrificed everything and was left with nothing. I realized that no amount of success could offset losing your life to your business."*
> —Jeff Soderberg, founder, STG

A Legacy

I have a personal goal of making a difference with others. In doing this, I have challenges to meet and contributions to make. The following are not all of my lifetime goals, but reflect more of the personal qualities that will make a difference to other people.

I would like to:

* Be patient when it's most difficult to do so
* Understand other people in their frame of reference
* Leave a legacy of positive words and deeds

Congratulations on Your Continuing Learning and Development

In today's competitive workplace, everyone should continue to learn. You are the person who is most responsible for your future, and your decision to expand your knowledge base is a positive one that will pay well-deserved dividends.

Growing a company takes planning and capable people who share a common purpose. I invite you and your professional staff to visit our Web site, salesleaders.com. We provide articles, reports, and resources for companies and work with leadership teams focusing on sustainable growth. I am sure you and your sales and leadership teams will also find many practical and useful ideas, from coaching and motivating employees to successful selling.

If you would like to receive a summary of the laws and key models of the book that you can print out and post, send an e-mail to laws@salesleaders.com.

Do you have an interesting or unique sales example you would like to share that shows how you or someone you know provided a high-value, innovative customer solution in an environment of rapid change? If so, please e-mail it to me at story@salesleaders.com. If I can use your example, I'll send you a release; sign it and send it back to me, and I'll post your example on the website, www.salesleaders.com.

BIBLIOGRAPHY

Books

Alessandra, Tony. *The Platinum Rule*. New York: Warner Books, 1998.

Baber, Michael. *How Champions Sell*. New York: Amacom, 1997.

Bennis, Warren, and Burt Nanus. *Leaders: The Strategy for Taking Charge* (2nd ed.). New York: HarperBusiness, 1997.

Christensen, Clayton M. *The Innovator's Dilemma*. New York: Harper-Business, 2000.

Coker, Darlene M., et al. *High Performance Sales Organizations: Creating Competitive Advantage in the Global Marketplace*. New York: McGraw-Hill, 2000.

DePree, Max. *Leadership Is an Art*. New York: Doubleday, 1990.

Gerber, Michael E. *Power Point Marketing One: Building a Small Business That Works*. Santa Rosa, Calif. 1994.

Good, Bill. *Prospecting Your Way to Sales Success*. New York: Scribner, 1997.

Hesselbein, Frances, et al., editors. *The Leader of the Future*. San Francisco: Jossey-Bass, 1996.

Hirschberg, Jerry. *The Creative Priority: Driving Innovation in the Real World*. New York: HarperAudio, 1998.

Hammond, John S., et al. *Smart Choices: A Practical Guide to Making Better Decisions*. Boston: Harvard Business School Press, 1999.

Kotter, John P. *Leading Change*. Boston: Harvard Business School Press, 1996.

Kouzes, James M., and Barry Z. Posner. *The Leadership Challenge: How to Get Extraordinary Things Done in Organizations*. San Francisco: Jossey-Bass, 1988.

Mattimore, Bryan W. *99% Inspiration: Tips, Tales & Techniques for Liberating Your Business Creativity.* New York: Amacom, 1993.

Moore, Geoffrey A. *Crossing the Chasm: Marketing and Selling High-Tech Products to Mainstream Customers.* New York: HarperBusiness, 1999.

Morrisey, George L., Thomas L. Sechrest (contributor), Wendy B. Warman, and Wendy S. Warman (contributor). *Loud and Clear: How to Prepare and Deliver Effective Business and Technical Presentations* (4th ed.). Reading, MA, Perseus Publishing, 1997.

Ott, Rick. *Creating Demand: Move the Masses to Buy Your Product, Service, or Idea.* Richmond, Va.: Ocean View Communications, 1999.

Peters, Thomas J. *The Circle of Innovation: You Can't Shrink Your Way to Greatness.* New York: Knopf, 1997.

Peterson, Doug, and Walter G. Meyer (contributor). *Going for the Green: Selling in the 21st Century.* Piney Flats, TN: LTI Publishing, 2002.

Pitino, Rick. *Success Is a Choice: Ten Steps to Overachieving in Business and Life.* New York: Broadway Books, 1997.

Porter, Michael, E. *Competitive Advantage: Creating and Sustaining Superior Performance.* New York: Free Press, 1985.

Prochaska, James O., et al. *Changing for Good.* New York: Morrow, 1994.

Rackham, Neil. *SPIN Selling.* New York: McGraw-Hill, 1988.

Ries, Al, and Jack Trout. *Positioning: The Battle for Your Mind.* New York: McGraw-Hill Trade, 2000.

Schultz, Howard, and Dori Jones Yang. *Pour Your Heart Into It: How Starbucks Built a Company One Cup At a Time.* New York: Hyperion, 1997.

Tracy, Brian. *Advanced Selling Strategies.* New York: Simon & Schuster, 1995.

Trout, Jack, with Steve Rivkin. *The New Positioning.* New York: McGraw-Hill, 1996.

Weiss, Alan. *Million Dollar Consulting.* New York: McGraw-Hill, 1992.

Wilson, Larry, and Hersch Wilson. *Play to Win! Choosing Growth over Fear in Work and Life.* Austin, TX: Bard Press, 1998.

Ziglar, Zig. *See You at the Top: 25th Anniversary Edition.* Gretna, LA: Pelican, 2000.

Periodicals

Anderson, James C., and James A. Narus. "Business Marketing: Understand What Customers Value." *Harvard Business Review* (November-December 1998): 53–65.

Ante, Spencer E. "The New Blue." *Business Week* (March 17, 2003): 80–88.

Bianco, Anthony, and Tom Lowry. "Can Dick Parsons Rescue AOL Time Warner?" *Business Week* (May 19, 2003): 86–96

Cooper, Ginger. *Customer Relationship Management* (November 2002): 34.

Kim, W. Chan, and Renee A. Mauborgne. "Value Innovation: The Strategic Logic of High Growth." *Harvard Business Review* (January-February 1997): 103–112.

Raskin, Andy. "Voulez-Vous—Completely Overhaul This Big, Slow Company and Start Making Some Cars that People Actually Want." *Business 2.0* (January 2002).

INDEX

Planning a sales meeting or special event?

Would you like to add a special touch to your meeting? Jim DeSena's high-energy, down-to-earth speeches have inspired thousands of people from diverse backgrounds to achieve the most life has to offer. He is a speaker who is continually sought after for his enthusiastic presentations at sales and management meetings, marketing conferences, and special events. He has advised close to two hundred Fortune 500 and growing companies and associations. Call 1-800-4321-WIN (1-800-432-1946) to find out how he can customize a program for you. Visit his website at www.salesleaders.com

Jim DeSena provides advice to organizations committed to growing their company and their employees. His areas of expertise are sales, leadership, and customer service. He helps clients develop compelling business missions, sell high-value, innovative customer solutions in an environment of rapid change, and provide award-winning customer service. Jim's research focus is on organizations that create long-term sustainable leadership, customer value, and growth. He has designed, developed, and delivered training, speaking, and consulting organizations throughout the United States and Canada. He is a former member of technical staff at Bell Laboratories and marketing executive with AT&T. He has an M.B.A. in management from New York University, an M.S. from Rutgers University, and a B.M.E. from the City College of New York.